RAF CHINOOK

1980 onwards (Marks HC-1 to HC-6)

COVER CUTAWAY: Boeing Chinook HC-1.

(Mike Badrocke)

First published in July 2015

A catalogue record for this book is available
from the British Library.

ISBN 978 0 85733 401 5

Library of Congress control no. 2014930891

Published by Haynes Publishing,
Sparkford, Yeovil,
Somerset BA22 7JJ, UK.
Tel: 01963 442030 Fax: 01963 440001
Int. tel: +44 1963 442030
Int. fax: +44 1963 440001
E-mail: sales@haynes.co.uk
Website: www.haynes.co.uk

Haynes North America Inc.,
861 Lawrence Drive, Newbury Park,
California 91320, USA.

Printed in the USA by Odcombe Press LP,
1299 Bridgestone Parkway, La Vergne,
TN 37086.

Acknowledgements

The author would like to thank all the pilots, crewmen and
engineers of Nos 7, 18 (B) and 27 Squadrons, RAF Odiham,
who helped with my research for this book. Many of those individuals
are mentioned in the chapters, while others provided anonymous
help, but all gave essential guidance through the complexities of
maintaining and flying Chinooks. (Any mistakes, however, are purely
my own.) A special mention must go to Flight Lieutenant Megan
Henderson (who made the whole research process possible,
and dealt with my endless requests), Flight Sergeant Mark Lilley,
Flight Sergeant John Chadwick (and all the other members of
the engineering team – see Chapter 7), Jay Myers (RAF External
Publications), Squadron Leader John McFall and Squadron Leader
Tony Field; and Flight Lieutenant Kyle Thomas for his extended
interview. I would also like to thank Jonathan Falconer, Senior
Commissioning Editor at Haynes Publishing, for his support
throughout this project.

RAF CHINOOK

1980 onwards (Marks HC-1 to HC-6)

Onwers' Workshop Manual

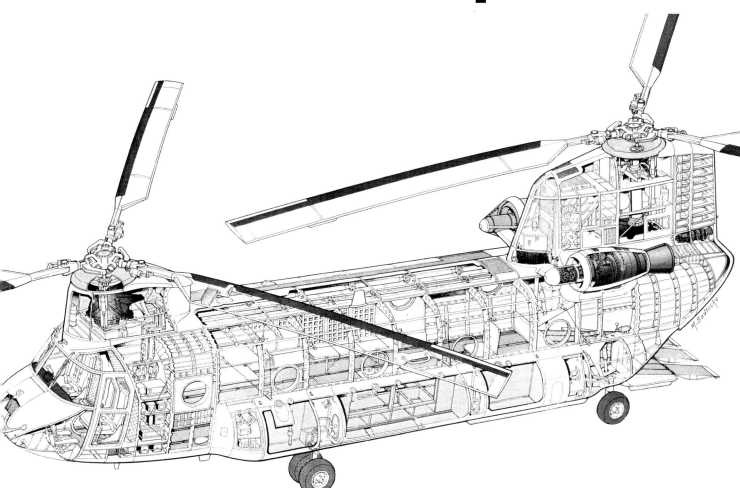

An insight into the design, construction and operation of the
RAF's tandem-rotor support helicopter

Chris McNab

Contents

OPPOSITE A pair of RAF Chinook HC-2 helicopters from 1310 Flight takes off from Camp Bastion airfield in Helmand, Afghanistan, as a US Air Force Blackhawk helicopter awaits its turn to land. *(Crown Copyright)*

Introduction

There are few helicopters as instantly recognisable as the Chinook. Mainly this familiarity results from the helicopter's unique layout – the twin rotors making it readily identifiable, even from distance. Then there's the issue of size. The Chinook is, quite frankly, a monster of a machine. Its fuselage measures nearly 50ft 9in (15.47m) in length from tip to tail and stands nearly 19ft (5.8m) tall from ground level to the centre of the rear rotor. Each three-blade rotor creates a turning circle 60ft (18.3m) in diameter, the two together producing a ferocious downblast to those beneath, while also providing the motive power to lift dozens of men and tons of cargo. The Chinook is therefore both physically and logistically arresting.

Yet there is another reason for the Chinook's familiarity – its ubiquity. From the Vietnam War to the present day, almost every major battlefield has thudded with the sound of the Chinook. Their missions have been of huge variety, ranging from the mundane to the lethal.

In their various guises Chinook missions have included resupply, troop deployments, medical evacuation (medevac), special forces (SF) insertions and extractions, reconnaissance, refuelling, aerial fire support and demonstration flights. Hundreds of thousands of soldiers around the world have experienced the comfort of hearing a Chinook approach, knowing that it represents food, mail from home, a trip to safety or the best chance that an injured comrade will get to medical help in time. While helicopters such as the Apache and the Cobra might steal some of the glamour of military helicopter aviation, it's the Chinook that represents the true battlefield workhorse.

This book is specifically focused on the Chinooks, and the men and women who pilot and maintain them, of the Royal Air Force (RAF), based in three squadrons – 7, 18 (B) and 27 – at RAF Odiham in Hampshire. As is the way of Haynes Manuals, it will give the reader a deep insight into the layout and technicalities of the RAF Chinooks. It will also, however, show the human dimension of these remarkable aircraft. As a true battlefield helicopter, often tasked to fly into decidedly 'hot' war zones, the Chinooks frequently find themselves within even small-arms range of the enemy. As such, the helicopter's crews experience a level of danger and a proximity to regular combat encountered by few types of aircrew. This book is as much a recognition of their bravery, and the dedication of those who keep these great machines flying, as it is of the helicopter itself.

BELOW Two HC-2 helicopters from 1310 Flight taking off from Camp Bastion airfield in Helmand, Afghanistan; the aircraft are part of the Joint Helicopter Force (Afghanistan) or JHF(A), a deployed tri-service unit from the Joint Helicopter Command. *(Crown Copyright)*

Chapter One

The Chinook story

The Chinook is a success story on many levels. Not only does it represent near-perfection in helicopter design, in terms of reliability and functionality, it has also made an inestimable contribution to battlefield logistics and tactics. Regardless of its users or its environment, the Chinook shows no signs of being outdated even after five decades of service.

OPPOSITE **Royal Marines from Alpha Company, 40 Commando, brace themselves against the downdraft from an incoming RAF Chinook helicopter during Operation DAAS 7B in Afghanistan, 7 December 2012.** *(Crown Copyright)*

ABOVE A dramatic image of HC-1 Chinook ZD575, seen flying in formation with a mix of Puma, Lynx and Gazelle helicopters. The helicopter was with 240 Operational Conversion Unit (OCU) until 1993, when it went to 18 Squadron. *(PRMAVIA Collection)*

BELOW A Chinook moves in with its centre hook extension ready to pick up a vehicular load. Unlike single-rotor helicopters that have to devote 15% of their power to the tail rotor, the Chinook can deliver all its force to lifting operations. *(PRMAVIA Collection)*

The Chinook story is an international narrative. Although the helicopter originated in the United States, with the Vertol company, it was subsequently owned and operated by 17 nations, including Japan and the United Kingdom (the two countries with the largest non-US fleets), Italy, South Korea, Spain, Taiwan, Canada, Morocco, Libya and Iran (in the days of the Imperial Iranian Air Force). Each country has put the helicopter through its own set of demands and operations, worthy of individual consideration. Here, however, we will discipline ourselves to the story of the helicopter's origins in the United States, its acquisition by the UK, and its subsequent development in RAF service.

OPPOSITE A Chinook flies in a humanitarian load to a supply depot in Pakistan. Digital assistance of the flight controls makes the Chinook extremely stable in the hover. *(PRMAVIA Collection)*

Twin-rotor development

The Chinook is a venerable machine, now with more than 50 years of operational service behind it, but twin-rotor helicopters have an even older ancestry. Some of the earliest conceptions of rotary-wing aircraft – Leonardo da Vinci's helical air screw (15th century) and Viscomte Gustave de Ponton d'Amecourt's fictional steam-powered *Albatross* (1863) – had multiple rotors, of sorts. During the early 20th century, when actual helicopters began to lift off the ground and not just in imagination, multiple rotors were the order of the day. The first was the Gyroplane No 1, designed by French brothers Jacques and Louis Breguet in 1907; the aircraft's four four-blade rotors lifted it to the dizzying altitude of 2ft (0.6m), but it was a start, and others soon followed. Landmarks included Dr George de Bothezat's 'Flying Octopus', featuring four six-bladed variable-pitch rotors, which became the US Army's first official helicopter in 1922, and the German Focke-Wulf Fw 61 of 1936, with twin counter-rotating rotors fitted on outriggers, a clumsy-looking design that nevertheless flew a world record distance of 143 miles (230km) at more than 11,000ft (3,352m) altitude and reached a speed of 76mph (122km/h).

Despite such adventures in multi-rotor helicopters, during the late 1930s helicopter design took a radically different direction at the hands of a seminal figure in the history of aircraft development – Igor Sikorsky. A Russian immigrant working in the United States, Sikorsky developed what would be the most enduring and familiar helicopter layout. Introduced by the Vought-Sikorsky aircraft company in 1939, the VS-300 featured a single top-mounted rotor, plus a small vertical rotor mounted on the tail to counteract the torque produced by the main rotor. As history now knows, the main rotor/tail rotor configuration became the standard design for hundreds of helicopters to this day, being efficient, cost-effective to produce and relatively straightforward to fly.

Yet the dual-rotor vision did not die out, offering as it did potential advantages in payload capacity, manoeuvrability and power (explained below). A key figure in this regard was Frank Nicholas Piasecki (1919–2008). A mechanical and aviation engineer from Philadelphia, Piasecki worked on the XR-1 dual-rotor helicopter project for the Platt-LePage company during the late 1930s, although he resigned over what he saw as flaws in the design. (The XR-1 prototypes experienced several crashes during testing, and Platt-LePage's contract with the US Air Force was cancelled at the end of World War Two.) At just 21 years old, Piasecki teamed up with friend and engineer

BELOW The Piasecki H-21 Shawnee first flew in 1952. Like the Chinook to come, it was a multi-mission tandem-rotor helicopter, and it saw US service into the mid-1960s. *(PRMAVIA Collection)*

Howard Venzie to create the PV Engineering Forum company in 1940, focusing on helicopter design. Their first two designs were the PV-1 and PV-2, both single-rotor helicopters but with some interesting innovations. The PV-1, for example, dispensed with the tail rotor in favour of a ducted fan system. The quality of the PV-2, furthermore, brought Piasecki to the attention of the US Navy, and the young designer (still just 24 years old) pitched the idea for a tandem-rotor helicopter known as the PV-3. It was the beginning of the journey towards the Chinook.

The PV-2 was not the only tandem-rotor helicopter around in the late 1940s and early 1950s. Other designs included the short-lived Rotorcraft XR-11 'Dragonfly' and the more successful McCullock MC-4/YH-30/Jovair 4E. Yet it was Piasecki's concepts that would go on to produce one of history's most influential helicopter types. Building on the experience of the PV-2, Piasecki developed the PV-3 to meet a US Navy requirement. This tandem-rotor machine had a main rotor diameter of 41ft (12.5m) and, powered by a 600hp Pratt & Whitney (P&W) engine, it was capable of hauling eight passengers and a 1,800lb (818kg) payload. Flight demonstrations were a success, and the US Navy adopted limited numbers of the production version, the HRP-1.

Here was a pivotal moment in Piasecki's career. The adoption of the HRP-1 proved the merit of the tandem-rotor concept, and Piasecki rode upon this momentum during the 1950s by developing further heavy-lift types. These were the HUP-1 and variants, carrier-capable helicopters performing various medevac, rescue, utility and combat (anti-submarine warfare) roles. Capability took a jump forward with the H-21 'workhorse' of 1952, best-known in its H-21C 'Shawnee' variant. Not only did the H-21 raise the bar considerably in terms of performance and payload, but it also helped pioneer the development of air-assault tactics in the Vietnam War (the first Shawnee deployments there began in 1961). Piasecki also upped the lift capacity of the type with what was, in 1953, the world's largest helicopter, the YH-16 'Transporter'. At 78ft (23.7m) long, the Transporter could carry 40 troops or 32 litters, or lift 14,000lb (6,363kg) of cargo. Although a test-flight crash in December 1955 led to the programme being cancelled, the

DUAL-ROTOR SYSTEMS AND TANDEM ROTOR FLIGHT

The obvious advantage of a dual-rotor helicopter is that of lifting power. A single-rotor helicopter loses some 15% of its power to the tail rotor, which purely serves as an anti-torque mechanism, compensating for the twist applied to the fuselage by the main rotor. In the case of a dual-rotor helicopter, both rotors are directly contributing to lift, providing advantages in both speed and cargo load. It should be noted, however, that there are several types of dual-rotor system. The Chinook is a tandem-rotor helicopter, meaning that the rotors are mounted one behind the other. Coaxial rotors feature two contra-rotating rotors mounted on the same shaft. Less common are intermeshing rotors, in which the rotors are mounted on separate rotor masts, but set at different angles to one another. Finally, there are transverse or lateral rotors, directional rotors mounted on the ends of wings/outriggers, as seen in modern aircraft such as the V-22 Osprey. This configuration essentially creates a type of vertical take-off and landing fixed-wing aircraft. In a tandem rotor system, forward flight is achieved by increasing the thrust of the aft rotary wing (via blade pitch adjustments) and decreasing the thrust of the forward blades, causing the aircraft to tilt nose down and move forward. Directional control is delivered by altering the plane of the rotor rotation, instructions to the rotors delivered via the cyclic stick or pedals. The helicopter will move towards the side of the downward tilt on the rotors.

BELOW The YH-16 was another design from Frank Piasecki. Only two were built, and a crash by one of them on a test flight in 1956 led to the project's cancellation. *(PRMAVIA Collection)*

Transport had embedded the idea of the very large, heavy-lift helicopter in military thinking.

Piasecki's contribution to the development of tandem-rotor helicopters, and therefore to the Chinook, is seminal. Yet it was another company, Vertol, which would pick up the dual-rotor idea and take it to its greatest perfection.

Enter Vertol

In the mid-1950s, the American Vertol Aircraft Corporation began a major fact-finding project. Their ultimate goal was to develop a military medium-lift helicopter that would satisfy the requirements of all four services: Army, Navy, Air Force and Marine Corps. They now had the advantage that gas-turbine technology was entering use, providing a more efficient power source than the reciprocating engines used in previous helicopters. Based on multiple questionnaires, Vertol acquired a demanding range of criteria, including rear-loading capability, the capacity to handle both personnel and cargo, simple field maintenance procedures (so the helicopter could be deployed close to the front line), simplicity in control, carrier capability and minimum downwash. What emerged from this process, in the late 1950s, was the Model 107, which would start to take the recognisable form of the Chinook. Development began in 1957, using Piasecki's H-21 and H-25 (a utility transport variant of the HUP-1) as the foundations for the design. A larger version was also produced, the Model 114, for heavier lift operations.

The key helicopter to emerge from the Model

107 development was the YHC-1A, which in turn was adapted for US Navy and Marine Corps use as the CH-46 Sea Knight and served from 1964 until 2015. Although smaller and with less lifting capacity than the Chinook, the Sea Knight is recognisably of the Chinook stable, and it would not be long before the US Army and Air Force would have a similar but more capable tandem-rotor helicopter in its inventory. For in 1958 the US Army issued a competition invitation for 'Weapon System SS471L', a new US Army medium transport helicopter. (There had been a fervent argument within the US Army about what type of helicopter it actually required, a light tactical transport or a heavy airlift vehicle, the specification issued being something of a compromise between the two.) A total of five prestigious US aviation companies entered the race, including Vertol, which expanded dramatically in the spring of 1960 when acquired by Boeing, combining the two companies' formidable expertise in aviation design.

Boeing-Vertol won the competition to become the developer, and they focused upon adapting the Model 114, now given the title YHC-1B. It would be a winning formula. Powered by two Lycoming T55-L5 turboshaft engines, powering huge three-bladed rotors, the YHC-1B went through a variety of prototypes between 1961 and 1963. After the first prototype was damaged in a ground accident, it was the second prototype (59-04983) that first took to the sky, on 21 September 1961. In July 1962 the US Army relabelled the YHC-1B as the YCH-47A, but it went into production as the CH-47A Chinook, first deliveries being made to the US Army between August 1962 and February 1963.

Proving ground

The CH-47A emerged into US service in the early stages of American involvement in Vietnam, thus the new helicopter was rapidly tested in an unforgiving combat arena. (All but 34 of the 349 Model As produced went to Vietnam.) Although the tactical and operational lessons were harsh (79 helicopters were lost, 34 to enemy action), the CH-47's functional value on the battlefield was immense. Its two Lycoming engines (at first the T-55-L5 then later the more powerful T55-L7) could lift the 50ft 9in (15.5m) fuselage plus a cargo of 33 troops or 24 litters, or a 10,000lb (4,454kg) payload. As a transport and utility aircraft it had few equals, whether deploying artillery pieces or ammunition out to remote firebases or medevacing wounded troops straight from the field back to aid stations. Four versions were even converted to the ACH-47A configuration (ACH = Attack Cargo Helicopter), fitted with multiple cannon, machine guns and rocket pods to provide gunship support around 'hot' landing zones.

Yet as good as the CH-47A was, there came the need for more power, better flight characteristics and increased cargo lift. So, on 9 September 1966, the CH-47B flew for the first time, powered by T-55-L7 engines

generating 2,850shp and with new, larger rotor blades, strakes on the rear fuselage (these imparted better stability to the aircraft during cruising flight) and enhanced M60 machine-gun armament. Some 108 of these were produced in 1967–68, but the type was quickly surpassed by the CH-47C model, deliveries of which began in 1968. Although initially using the same power plant as the CH-47B, the CH-47C had larger fuel tanks (with improved crash protection), fibreglass-strengthened rotor blades and an uprated transmission. A total of 288 of these were produced from 1968 to 1985, and sales to foreign states included Australia, Canada, Greece, Iran, Morocco, South Korea and, crucially, the United Kingdom. For now the British began their long and fruitful relationship with the Chinook.

ABOVE One of the early Vertol 107 demonstrations in the United States. The Model 107 also served as a 25-passenger civilian helicopter, as well as becoming a US Navy and Marine Corps assault helicopter. *(PRMAVIA Collection)*

LEFT A Boeing-Vertol CH-46 Sea Knight, in service with the US Marine Corps aboard the USS *Coronado*, an amphibious transport dock vessel. Like the Chinook, the Sea Knight was a highly successful design, only retired from service in 2004. *(PRMAVIA Collection)*

ABOVE The Bristol
Belvedere was an early
British tandem-rotor
design, developed by
the Bristol Aeroplane
Company and used
in service by the RAF
from 1961 to 1969.
(PRMAVIA Collection)

Early British variants

The British were already familiar with the
tandem-rotor helicopter before it even
began making Chinook purchases. Between
1961 and 1969 the RAF had operated a fleet
of Bristol Type 192 Belvederes. The Belvedere
was actually based on earlier helicopters
designed for naval use; the naval contracts
were cancelled, and by consequence the Type
192 was less than optimally designed for army
utility and transport purposes. The Belvedere
had a load capacity of 6,000lb (2,727kg) and
could transport 18 fully armed troops, but it
had poor loading characteristics (there was
no rear door, and the main cargo door was
4ft (1.2m) above the ground) and was inferior
to the US helicopter in terms of performance.
Thus when the RAF looked around for a decent
replacement for the Belvedere, the Chinook
caught its attention, rather than reinventing the
wheel with a new design.

Early British acquisition of the Chinook was
rather farcical. In March 1967, the Ministry
of Defence (MoD) placed an order for 15
CH-47Bs, to be known in British usage as the
HC-1. The order was promptly cancelled in
a review of defence spending in November,
however, so the British adoption of the Chinook

was be delayed by more than a decade.
For the next ten years it was the single-rotor
Westland Wessex that formed the backbone of
the British Army's transport and utility capability,
but by the late 1970s the need for something
of greater muscle was becoming apparent. The
requirement for a Wessex replacement was
announced in 1978, with the US CH-47C to be
adopted, again with the designation of HC-1.
Thirty-three Chinooks were ordered with T55-L-
11E engines, triple cargo hooks, a single-point
pressure refuelling system and a rotor brake.
Later the HC-1s would also receive aluminium
and glass fibre rotor blades (the American
blades were initially all-metal), these helicopters
being designated the HC-1B.

The first RAF Chinooks were received
in 1980, operating out of RAF Odiham
in Hampshire, first with 240 Operational
Conversion Unit (OCU) then, from August
1981, with No 18 (Bomber) Squadron. The
HC-1s would serve with the RAF and Army,
supporting all Services throughout the 1980s.
Five were sent to the Falklands during the
conflict there in 1982, although most were
lost when their transporter ship, the *Atlantic
Conveyor*, was hit by an Exocet missile. They
also served in the First Gulf War (1990–91),
providing heavy lift for front-line British troops

in Kuwait and Iraq. During the 1980s, however, the Americans had developed a new improved mark of the Chinook, the CH-47D, planning for which began in the aftermath of the Vietnam War. The CH-47D was developed through modification of existing A, B and C models, and production, which began in 1982, saw 444 helicopters manufactured to the 'D' standard and two new-built, all delivered to the US Army between 1980 and 1985.

The CH-47D brought a raft of improvements to what was now a tried and tested air vehicle. The modifications included:

- Uprated transmissions and more powerful L-712 (late L-714A) engines.
- Lift capability of 25,000lb (11,363kg).
- Composite rotor blades.
- Improved electrical systems and hydraulics.
- Triple cargo hooks.
- Enhanced avionics and communication systems.
- Advanced flight control system.

RIGHT HC-1 ZD575 hovers over a Land Rover while infantrymen attach the vehicle to the helicopter's centre hook, which has a 28,000lb (12,727kg) capacity. *(PRMAVIA Collection)*

- Redesigned cockpit to decrease pilot workload.
- Large air intake for transmission cooling.

The CH-47D provided the RAF with the best option for upgrading their Chinook fleet. Between 1992 and 1995 the HC-1s were returned to Boeing in the United States, for upgrading to the HC-2 standard. Some new-build HC-2 Chinooks were also ordered during the 1990s: three standard HC-2s and six HC-2As, the latter featuring a strengthened and adapted front fuselage for fitment of an aerial refuelling probe.

ABOVE A Chinook seen flying over a desert region of Afghanistan in 2009. The forward door is removed to give the crew maximum visibility and threat awareness. *(PRMAVIA Collection)*

The winning formula offered by the Chinook led to other, more specialist, RAF orders during the 1990s. Specifically, this was the HC-3, a helicopter dedicated to SF mission support. Here was one of the less auspicious projects in the RAF Chinook's otherwise inspiring career. The HC-3 was based on the US special ops MH-47E, which featured enhanced terrain-following/terrain-avoidance radar systems (and corresponding cockpit modifications) to enable the helicopter to deliver more nimble infiltrations and exfiltrations, plus enhanced fuel capacity for longer-range missions (the HC-3 is instantly distinguished from the other marks by its prominent fuel 'fat tanks' running along the lower fuselage). Other Chinooks could achieve extended range through fitting internal auxiliary tanks in the cargo hold, but such fitment meant losing useful logistics capability. Ordered in 1995, and built to spec by Boeing, the HC-3 helicopters were delivered for service in 2001, at a cost of $259 million.

Now the problems began. The MoD was unable to certify the avionics software for airworthiness, specifically relating to instrument-only flying. (The contracts for the helicopters omitted a clause requiring access to the software source code; when Boeing was unable to provide this, the helicopters could

ABOVE An HC-2 makes a dramatic nose-down manoeuvre; the power plant of the HC-2 was the Textron Lycoming T55-L-712F. *(PRMAVIA Collection)*

RIGHT An HC-3 at Odiham, distinguished by the extended-range bulge tanks running along the side of the airframe. *(PRMAVIA Collection)*

RIGHT HC-3s in storage, their rotor blades removed from the forward pylons. The HC-3 procurement was one of the most difficult episodes in recent MoD history. *(PRMAVIA Collection)*

not be certified in the UK.) The result was that the helicopters ended up in extremely expensive storage, only able to fly in ideal visual conditions. Various solutions were sought, but in 2007 it was decided that the HC-3s would be reverted to the same cockpit standard as the HC-2/2A variant, so they could take their full place in the RAF's Chinook fleet, at a total cost (including the original purchase price) of some £500 million.

RIGHT Conducting operations as part of Operation *Herrick* in 2006, this Chinook is making an ammunition lift from the centre hook. Note the Minigun-armed crewman in the starboard doorway. *(PRMAVIA Collection)*

BELOW From beneath the starboard external rescue hoist, a crewman keeps watch during manoeuvres; the starboard door is a two-part affair, and the top section can be opened for improved visibility. *(PRMAVIA Collection)*

7 Squadron – (Motto: *Per diem, per noctem* – 'By day and by night'). No 7 Squadron has a history stretching back to 1914, principally as a bomber squadron. In September 1982, however, it reformed as a helicopter squadron equipped with Chinook HC-1s, receiving HC-2s in the 1990s.

18 Squadron – (Motto: *Animo et fide* – 'With courage and faith'). Like 7 Squadron, 18 Squadron also has a World War One vintage, but was flying helicopters (Westland Wessex) from 1965 to 1980. It reformed with Chinooks in 1981 (making it the first RAF Chinook squadron), but lost three of its machines when the *Atlantic Conveyor* was sunk during the Falklands War. Having spent much of the 1980s and 1990s in Germany, 18 Squadron moved in to RAF Odiham in 1997.

27 Squadron – (Motto: *Quam celerrime ad astra* – 'With all speed to the stars'). Formed in 1915, 27 Squadron came late to Chinooks, giving up its Tornado fighters for the helicopters in 1993, at first as a reserve squadron but gaining full squadron status in 1998.

BELOW Two Chinooks in flight together, seen at RAF Odiham, the home base for all RAF Chinooks. *(PRMAVIA Collection)*

Although the HC-3 incident was a very difficult time in the history of Chinook procurement, the sterling work of the RAF Chinooks and their crews continued. And there was indeed no shortage of work to do, courtesy of Nos 7, 18 and 27 Squadrons based at Odiham. Operational commitments included major deployments to Bosnia and Kosovo throughout the 1990s in support of humanitarian and peacekeeping efforts, and evacuation ops in Sierra Leone and the Lebanon in 2000 and 2006 respectively. Most visible, however, have been Chinook's prolific use in the wars in Iraq and Afghanistan since 2001. In this most demanding of theatres, the Chinook has been tested to its limits in all manner of climatic and tactical situations.

What the trials of these conflicts have proven is that the essential design of the Chinook is just as relevant to the battlefields of today as it was to those of the 1960s and 1970s. Yet at the same time the Chinook has received numerous upgrades and modifications that have kept it responsive to modern threat environments, from its defensive suites through to its avionics, largely in response to Urgent Operational Requirements (UORs). For example, in 2003 eight HC-2 aircraft received significant capability

BELOW With rotors and forward and aft pylons removed, the Chinook can be transported internally in aircraft such as the USAF C-5 Galaxy, seen here. (PRMAVIA Collection)

upgrades in the form of a night-enhancement package (NEP), consisting of a nose-mounted forward-looking infrared (FLIR) system, display NVG and moving map. Yet piecemeal modifications were not the most satisfactory route to upgrading the Chinook, thus in 2008 a major upgrade programme, known as Project Julius, was initiated.

Project Julius and beyond

Project Julius essentially focuses its efforts on opposite ends of the Chinook. At the front, the existing HC-2/2As and HC-3s are receiving an entirely new digitised cockpit, replacing the analogue cockpit with which generations of pilots had become so familiar. At the rear, the Chinooks are receiving more powerful T55-L-714A engines, to replace the T55-L-712F. The overall aim of the Julius upgrades, which will be run out through all 46 Chinooks of the RAF fleet, is not only to make them easier to fly (in terms of reducing the pilot workload), but also to provide the motive power to cope with operations demanding higher altitudes or greater lift demands. Upgraded HC-2/2As are designated HC-4s, while the HC-3s that have been through the process become HC-5s. First flight of an HC-4 took place at Gosport on 9 December 2010, and gradually the other Chinooks of the fleet are transiting through the upgrade system, with many going out to operational roles in Afghanistan.

The Chinook story is nearly up to date. Yet at the time of writing another exciting variant of the RAF Chinook is being introduced into service. This is the HC-6, which the MoD confirmed in August 2011 as a new-build purchase with Boeing. Essentially, the HC-6 is the American

OPPOSITE Another Odiham Chinook: the under-nose searchlight on this HC-4 is illuminated just to the right of the forward-looking infrared (FLIR) turret. *(PRMAVIA Collection)*

BELOW The real rationale for the Chinook lies in what it can carry, as much as how it can fly. Here a HC-2 deploys an infantry unit from the rear ramp during an exercise in September 2000. *(PRMAVIA Collection)*

CH-47F (the latest in the line of the US helicopters is the MH-47G).

The CH-47F was a major upgrade programme that began in 2003, which was aimed to keep the US fleet of nearly 500 Chinooks fit for service until 2030. As with Project Julius, much of the modification process has focused on the cockpit. The CH-47F features the Rockwell Collins digital cockpit allied to the common avionics architecture system (CAAS), featuring multi-function displays, moving map displays, digital modem, a BAE Systems digital advanced flight control system (DAFCS) plus enhanced data transfer systems for storing and transferring mission flight data. Moving from the software to the hardware, the CH-47F has also received structural modifications to the cockpit, cabin, pylon, ramp and aft section, as well as improved vibration-control systems (the Chinook can be a bone-shaker, depending on the variant) via its 'monolithic airframe' construction, meaning that the airframe is built in one large piece, rather than many pieces riveted together.

Field feedback on the CH-47F is enthusiastic, and the RAF versions will be received in the UK by 2015. Although the HC-6 will obviously be a close model of the CH-47F, the avionics and much of the mission-specific equipment will be modified for British use, including incorporating the Thales TopDeck system that is part of the Julius upgrade. What aircraft such as the HC-4 and HC-6 mean, is that the Chinook will remain a familiar sight to British troops for the next two decades, whether in peace or war. A more detailed look at what makes the helicopter such a success will be pursued in the next chapter.

RIGHT **The Chinook can put down on virtually any flat surface big enough to accommodate its fuselage and rotor diameter, here a Royal Navy aircraft carrier.** *(PRMAVIA Collection)*

Chapter Two

Anatomy of the Chinook

The Chinook is designed for maximum battlefield utility, in terms of performance, tactical versatility and durability. Its tandem-rotor construction provides superb lift capabilities for handling a variety of material and human loads, plus it supplies an astonishing degree of manoeuvrability for an aircraft of its size.

OPPOSITE A view down through the cabin of the Chinook, out the rear ramp door. Note the foldable seating arranged against the side of the cabin – there are 16 seats on the starboard side and 17 on the port side. Also note the pipe running up the sides and the roof of the cabin; this relates to fitting the extended-range fuel tank system. *(Author)*

RIGHT The combining transmission, which takes the power of the engines and sends that power at a reduced shaft speed to the forward and aft transmissions. *(Author)*

The most obvious construction feature of the Chinook, the one that makes it stand out from the crowd, is its tandem-rotor layout, the rotors mounted on forward and aft pylons with the twin turboshaft engines straddling the aft pylon. The aft pylon is the highest point of the helicopter, at 18ft 11in (5.77m), and other dimensions are equally impressive. From nose to the back of the aft pylon, the Chinook stretches 50ft 9in (15.47m – by way of comparison the RAF's Puma helicopter is 46.2ft/14.08m), and the distance between the forward and aft landing gears is 22.5ft (6.85m). The rotation circumference of each rotor blade is 60ft (18.28m), with 38ft 11in (11.85m) between the two rotor hubs. The upshot of all these dimensions is that the Chinook, including the physical space its rotors occupy, is 98ft 11in (30.15m) long, making it one of the largest battlefield helicopters around.

Set beneath and in front of the forward rotor pylon is the cockpit area, a workspace for the pilot and co-pilot. The nose of the aircraft, projecting out just beneath the feet of the pilots, houses wheel brakes and directional pedals, slide slip ports, pitot tube (for measuring air speed), radar warning antenna and (on some marks) a forward-looking infrared system (FLIR).

The engines, rotor systems and cockpit essentially comprise the 'flying' aspect of the Chinook. Yet the operational versatility of the Chinook largely revolves around the empty space it offers in terms of the cargo area, housed within the main body of the fuselage. The internal load capacity of the HC-2 is 17,960lb (8,164kg), but there are also three external cargo hooks: a 28,000lb (12,727kg) capacity central hook and two 20,000lb (9,090kg) capacity fore and aft hooks. In addition to handling cargo internally, the helicopter can also be configured to transport 54 combat-ready soldiers or 23 stretchers, for medical evacuation operations. Access to the helicopter interior is principally through the full width cargo ramp at the rear of the aircraft, or the starboard side cabin door. Running along the lower sides of the fuselage, in the distinctive 'bulges' (far more prominent in the HC-5), are the fuel tanks, each side of the aircraft having a main fuel tank and fore and aft auxiliary tanks. Supporting the whole helicopter during landing is the twin landing gear: two two-wheel landing gear at the front, and steerable single-wheel landing gear at the rear.

This rapid overview of the Chinook does the

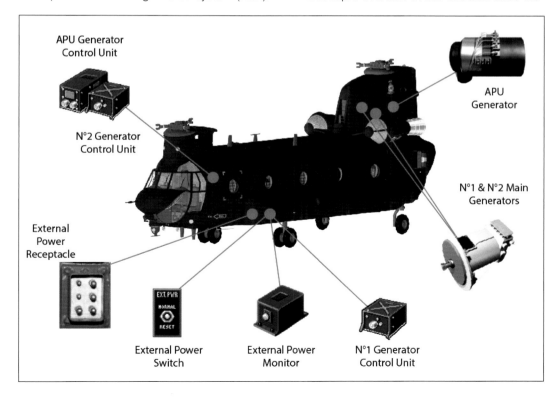

APU Generator
Control Unit

N°2 Generator
Control Unit

External
Power
Receptacle

EXT.PWR
NORMAL
RESET

External Power
Switch

External Power
Monitor

N°1 Generator
Control Unit

APU
Generator

N°1 & N°2 Main
Generators

LEFT A diagram showing the location of the Chinook's AC power generators, monitors, switches and units; the APU generator is responsible for delivering the power from the APU to the utility and hydraulic systems, when the rotors are not turning. *(Crown Copyright)*

Boeing Vertol Chinook HC-1. *(Mike Badrocke)*

1 FM homing aerials
2 Pitot tubes
3 Nose compartment access hatch
4 Vibration absorber
5 IFF aerial
6 Windscreen panels
7 Windscreen wipers
8 Instrument panel glare shield
9 Rudder pedals
10 Yaw sensing ports (automatic flight control system)
11 Downward vision window
12 Pilot's footboards
13 Collective pitch control column
14 Cyclic pitch control column
15 Co-pilot's seat
16 Centre instrument console
17 Pilot's seat
18 Glideslope aerial
19 Forward transmission housing fairing
20 Cockpit overhead window
21 Doorway from main cabin
22 Cockpit emergency exit doors
23 Sliding side window panel
24 Cockpit bulkhead
25 Vibration absorber
26 Cockpit door release handle
27 Radio and electronics racks
28 Sloping bulkhead
29 Stick boost actuators
30 Stability augmentation system actuators
31 Forward transmission mounting structure

32 Windscreen washer reservoir
33 Rotor control hydraulic jack
34 Forward transmission gearbox
35 Rotor head fairing
36 Forward rotor head mechanism
37 Pitch change control levers
38 Blade drag dampers
39 Glassfibre rotor blades
40 Titanium leading edge capping with de-icing provision
41 Rescue hoist/winch
42 Forward transmission aft fairing
43 Hydraulic system modules
44 Control levers
45 Front fuselage frame and stringer construction
46 Emergency exit window
47 Forward end of cargo floor
48 Fuel tank fuselage side fairing
49 Battery
50 Electrical system equipment bay
51 HF/SSB aerial cable
52 Stretcher rack (up to 24 stretchers)
53 Cabin window panel
54 Cabin heater duct outlet
55 Troop seats stowed against cabin wall
56 Cabin roof synchronising shaft
57 Formation keeping lights
58 Rotor blade cross-section
59 Blade balance and tracking weight socket

60 Leading edge anti-erosion strip
61 Fixed tab
62 Fuselage skin plating
63 Maintenance walkway
64 Transmission tunnel access doors
65 VHF/AM – UHF/AM aerial
66 Troop seating, up to 44 troops
67 Cargo hook access hatch
68 VOR aerial
69 Cabin lining panels
70 Control runs
71 Main transmission shaft
72 Shaft couplings
73 Centre fuselage construction
74 Centre aisle seating (optional)

75 Main cargo floor: 1,440cu ft (40.78m^3) cargo volume
76 Ramp-down 'dam' for water-borne operations
77 Ramp hydraulic jack
78 Engine bevel drive gearbox
79 Transmission combining gearbox
80 Rotor brake
81 Transmission oil tank

82 Engine drive shaft fairing
83 Engine intake screen
84 Starboard engine nacelle
85 Oil coolers
86 Cooling air intake grilles
87 Oil cooling air fan
88 Fire extinguisher bottles
89 Fan drive shaft
90 Cooling air outlet louvres
91 Maintenance step
92 Aft pylon construction
93 Swash plate fixed link
94 Aft rotor drive shaft
95 Aft rotor bearing mounting
96 Rotor head fairing
97 Aft rotor head mechanism
98 Main rotor blades, glassfibre construction
99 Rotor control hydraulic jack

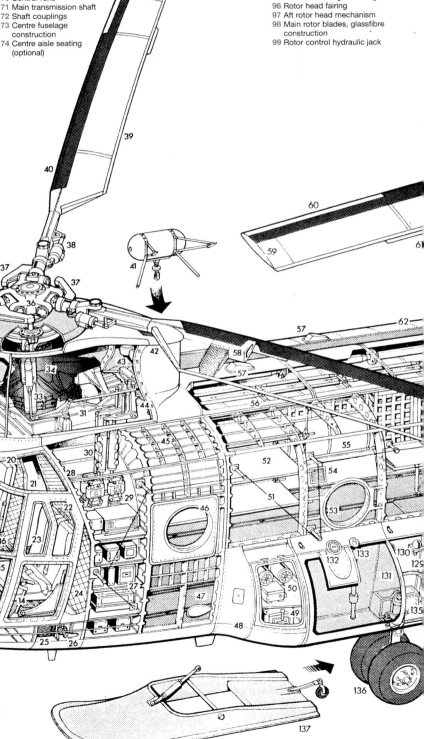

100 Hydraulic filters and
     reservoirs
101 Pylon aft fairing
     construction
102 Blunt trailing edge section
103 Tail navigation light
104 Solar T62-T2A1 auxiliary
     power unit (APU)
105 APU-driven generators
106 Maintenance walkways
107 Engine exhaust duct
108 Lycoming T55-L-11E
     turboshaft engine
109 Detachable engine
     cowlings
110 Rear fuselage frame and
     stringer construction
111 Rear cargo doorway
112 Ramp extensions
113 Cargo ramp, lowered
114 Ramp ventral strake
115 Fuselage side fairing aft
     extension
116 Ramp control lever

117 Ramp hydraulic jack
118 Rear undercarriage shock
     absorber
119 Undercarriage leg strut
120 Single rear wheels
121 Rear wheel optional ski
     fitting
122 Maintenance step
123 Rear crashproof fuel tank
124 Fuel tank interconnections
125 Ventral strake
126 Main crashproof fuel tank;
     total system capacity 1,042
     US gal (3,944 litres)
127 Floor beam construction
128 Fuel tank attachment joint
129 Fuel system piping

130 Fire suppression bottles
131 Forward crashproof fuel
     tank
132 Fuel filler caps
133 Fuel capacity transmitters
134 ADF sense aerial rail
135 Front undercarriage
     mounting
136 Twin forward mainwheels
137 Forward wheel optional ski
     fitting
138 Triple cargo hook system,
     forward and rear cargo
     hooks: 20,000lb (9,080kg)
     capacity
139 Main cargo hook: 28,000lb
     (12,712kg) capacity

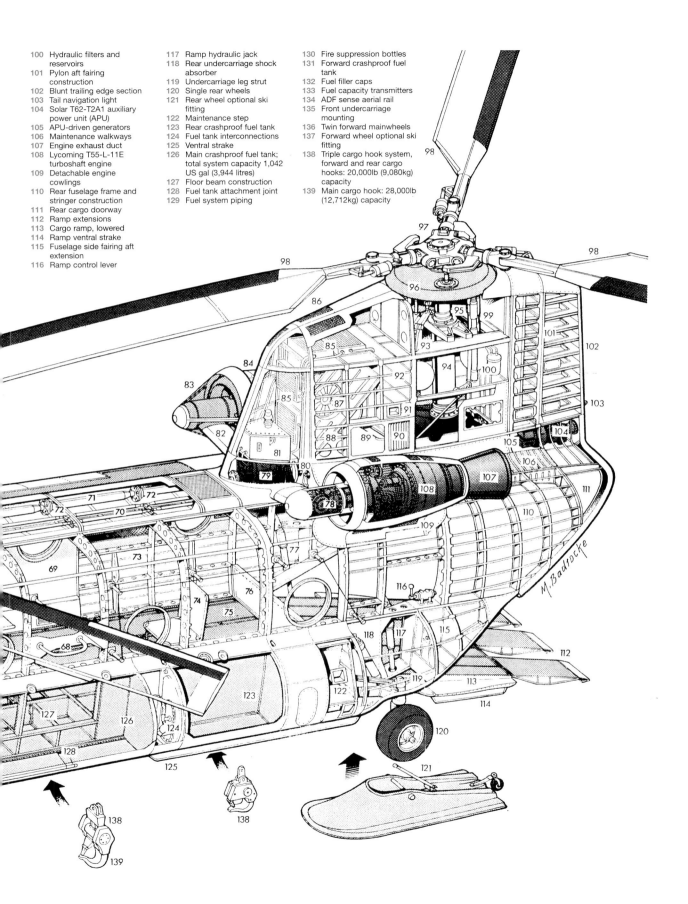

machine justice in one way, by emphasising the overall structural simplicity of the machine. The Chinook is built to be reliable in environments that by their very nature present a fundamental challenge to that reliability. At the same time, the Chinook is a machine adapted to the complexities of modern warfare, acquiring various sophistications over the years that help to improve its survivability, which we will now study in more detail.

Main rotor system

The defining characteristic of the Chinook is its tandem-rotor system, with three blades per rotor. Each rotor is 3ft (90cm) wide and 29.5ft (8.9m) long, consisting of a D-shaped titanium spar with a honeycomb fibreglass

aerofoil section and a Nomex fairing assembly fitted to the spar. Titanium and nickel erosion caps protect the leading edge of the blade, the part most vulnerable to impact erosion from airborne particles. If there is any doubt about the necessity of such protection, an observer only need witness the striking luminous halo effect generated by the rotors as they slash through a dust cloud in low-light conditions. (The phenomenon, properly known as the Kopp–Etchels Effect, is created when metal particles are dispersed into the air and ignited by impact with the sand particles.) Lightning protection is provided by each blade having two lightning cables running to the rotor head.

The rotor head itself consists of a hub connected to three pitch-varying shafts via three horizontal hinge pins, which permit the natural up-and-down movement of the blade during flight (known as 'blade flapping'). Set coaxially over the pitch-varying shafts are pitch-varying housings; the rotor blades are attached to these housings by hinge pins. Chinook engineers also speak with reverence about the 'Jesus nut', the castellated nut that holds the rotor on to the rotor shaft; the religious nickname comes from the implication that a failure of the nut in flight will almost certainly result in a rapid journey to the afterlife, given that the rotors will be spinning at up to 225rpm.

The ability to control both the individual pitch of each blade and the entire rotor disc attitude (its angle in relation to the blade's horizontal plane), is what enables it to fly. The US Army's *Operator's Manual for Army CH-47D Helicopter* (Technical Manual 1-1520-240-10) clarifies how the individual blade pitch changes during a rotor rotation (known as cyclic-pitch change) and the pitch change of the entire rotor (known as collective-pitch change) are made: 'Blade pitch changes are accomplished by three pitch-varying links connected from the rotating rim of the swashplate to the pitch-varying housing on each rotor blade. Cyclic pitch changes are accomplished by tilting the swashplate.'

BELOW A cross-sectional diagram of one of the Chinook's rotor blades, clearly showing its D-spar configuration and frontal weighting. Note the nose cap, to protect it from the erosive effects of air particles. *(Crown Copyright)*

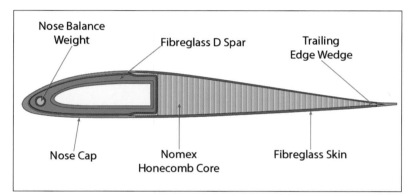

Nose Balance Weight

Fibreglass D Spar

Trailing Edge Wedge

Nose Cap

Nomex Honecomb Core

Fibreglass Skin

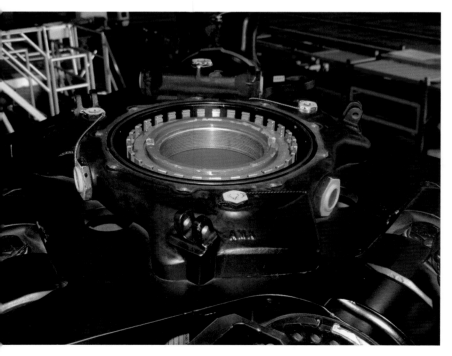

LEFT The 'Jesus nut', the unit that fixes the rotor blades to the rotor head. Despite the huge loads placed on this component, failures of the nut are extremely rare as long as everything is fitted properly. *(Author)*

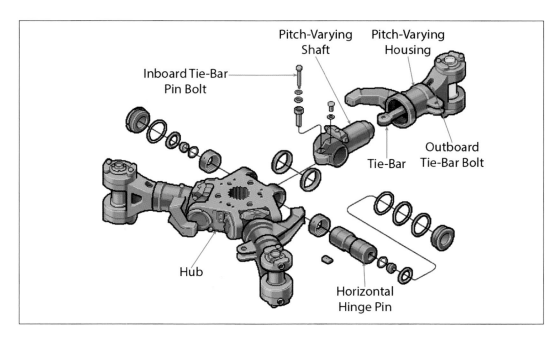

Pitch-Varying
Shaft

Pitch-Varying
Housing

Inboard Tie-Bar
Pin Bolt

Outboard
Tie-Bar Bolt

Tie-Bar

Hub

Horizontal
Hinge Pin

Collective pitch changes are accomplished by vertical movement of the swashplate. Combined collective and cyclic pitch change result from the combined control inputs by the pilot' (2-8-1). To give the Chinook a level orientation when it is in flight, the front rotor is angled forward at 9°, while the rear rotor is set at a 4° angle.

Of course, the fact that the Chinook has two rotor heads, not one, means that the blades have to work meaningfully and safely together to deliver efficient flight. The intermeshing rotors turn in different directions and at different angles; the fact that the blades are counter-rotating also reduces the torque that would be generated by a single-rotor helicopter (the Chinook has a 60/40 split on torque between the forward and aft rotors). The synchronicity required by the Chinook's rotor system is achieved by running both rotors through a single power plant (composed of the twin engines set on the rear pylon) and via a complicated transmission system. Note that each

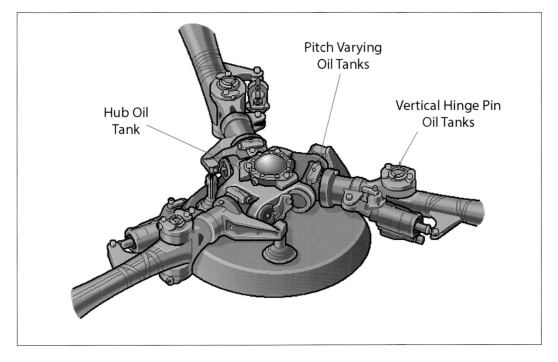

Pitch Varying
Oil Tanks

Vertical Hinge Pin
Oil Tanks

Hub Oil
Tank

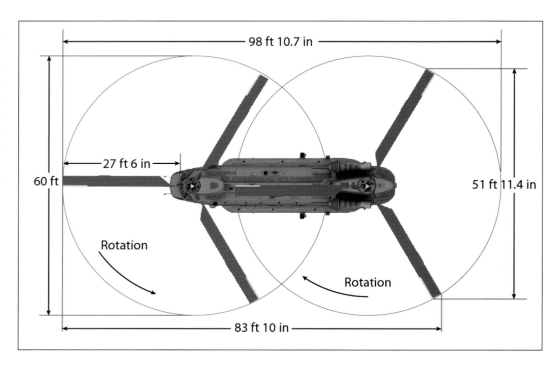

of the two engines are not powering separate rotors. In fact, the Chinook could suffer failure of one of the engines, and the remaining good engine could still drive the twin rotors in most flight conditions.

Hydraulics and the APU

Before moving on to examine the cockpit area of the Chinook, it is worth looking in more detail at the hydraulics systems aboard the helicopter. Essentially there are three hydraulic supply systems in action. The No 1 and No 2

flight control systems are those responsible for powering the flight controls; they operate at 3,000psi or 1,500psi, depending on the system to which they are providing functionality. The utility hydraulic system has a very broad range of functions within the aircraft, including powering the wheel brakes, steering actuator, hydraulic cargo door motor, swivel locks, centring cams, ramp actuating cylinders, actuators for the hooks, rescue winch control valve, two engine starters, power transfer units (PTUs) and the APU. From wheel braking to engine starts, therefore, the utility hydraulic system provides

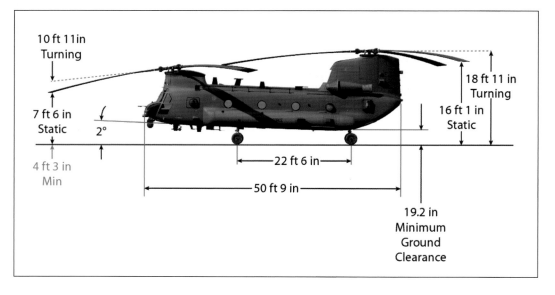

RIGHT A simple troop warning-bell system enables the crew to give straightforward instructions to troops on board and other military personnel, essential given the noise levels aboard the aircraft. *(Author)*

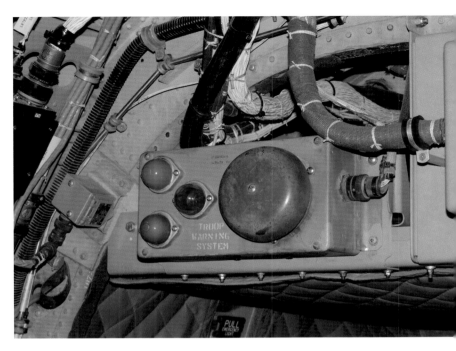

the power for the Chinook to perform its critical functions. It should be pointed out that when the engines are not running, the APU delivers the power for the utility hydraulic system, but once the rotors are turning the aft transmission pump takes over.

The T62-T-2B APU is located in the aft cabin, just above the ramp. This small unit consists of a gas turbine engine, hydraulic motor pump, fuel control, accessory drive and an AC generator. In terms of functions, the APU is there to supply power to the aircraft electrical systems when the main generators are not on line, while the APU's hydraulic pump enables main engine start and ground checks by providing pressure for the utility and hydraulic systems. Also mounted near the APU is the electronic sequencing unit (ESU). Essentially this unit monitors the performance of the APU, particularly its running speed and exhaust gas temperatures. If either of these functions exceeds parameters programmed into the ESU, then the ESU can shut the APU down.

Sergeant John Chadwick, a senior engineer on the Chinook, describes the purpose of the APU in layman's terms: 'You need quite a chunk of power to start the engines, so to try to do that with a battery and a small jar of stored pressure you wouldn't get them going. Yet that battery and that small jar of stored pressure will get the APU going, and once the APU is going that has its own generator and its own hydraulic pressure pump, and those will do the job.'

Cockpit, flight control systems and avionics

I t is in the cockpit that the bulk of the Chinook's technology is concentrated, in a bewildering (to the uninitiated) array of dials, displays screens, panels, knobs and switches. The layout and technology of the Chinook's cockpit naturally varies somewhat according to the mark, particularly in the case of the Mk 4

and later marks, but essentially the basic layout remains the same. There are two seats in the cockpit, one for the pilot (usually on the right) and the other for the co-pilot (usually on the left). The seats themselves are fully adjustable for forward, aft, vertical and reclining planes, and they are also armoured with both fixed and adjustable ceramic armour panels. These panels are fitted under the back and bottom seat cushions and on the outboard side of the seat, with the option of a hinged shoulder panel, also on the outboard side. The pilot and co-pilot have vision forward via three main forward windows, plus two curved windows wrapping

BELOW The pilot's and co-pilot's principal flight controls: the cyclic (for lateral and longitudinal control), the collective (for vertical control) and the pedals for directional control. *(Crown Copyright)*

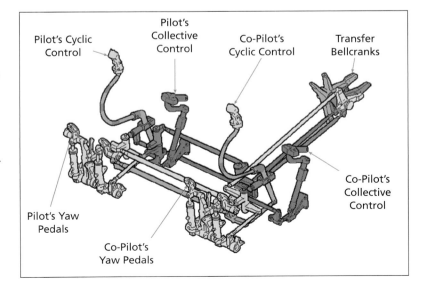

Pilot's Cyclic Control

Pilot's Collective Control

Co-Pilot's Cyclic Control

Transfer Bellcranks

Pilot's Yaw Pedals

Co-Pilot's Yaw Pedals

Co-Pilot's Collective Control

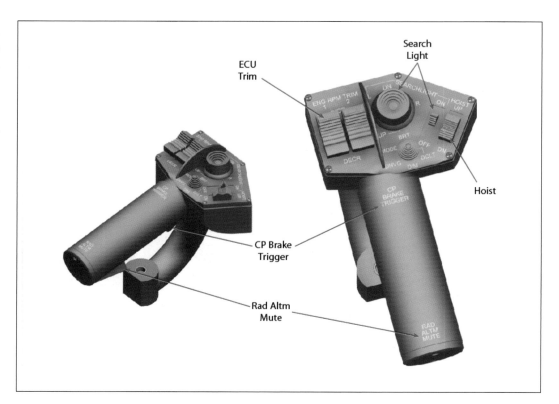

RIGHT A close-up of the HC-2 collective. As well as controlling elevation, the collective also has certain practical controls, such as for the searchlight and hoists. The control can be set in place with a magnetic brake. *(Crown Copyright)*

around the nose beneath the level of the pilot's/co-pilot's feet. Of the three upper windows, the pilot's and co-pilot's windows are fitted with electric de-icing and de-fogging equipment, while the centre window has de-fogging only.

Flying the helicopter involves the combined manipulation of the cyclic control stick (the joystick directly in front of the pilot between their knees), the collective (known to Americans as the thrust lever) and the pedals. The collective

BELOW The helicopter's cyclic control. The stick trim button allows fine adjustment of attitude, while other switches and buttons give the pilot final control over comms, defensive measures and cargo release. *(Crown Copyright)*

is essentially responsible for the vertical lift or descent of the helicopter – raising the collective increases the pitch, and therefore lift, of the rotors, while lowering it decreases the pitch and the altitude. For lateral and longitudinal flight, the cyclic stick is the primary control. Here the US Army's field manual clarifies the technicalities: 'Each cyclic stick is used for lateral and longitudinal control of the helicopter. Moving the cyclic stick to the right causes the helicopter to roll to the right in flight. Moving the stick to the left causes the opposite movement. When moving the cyclic stick forward, the pitch of the fwd [*sic*] rotor blades is decreased collectively, while the pitch of the aft rotor blades is increased collectively, thus causing a nose-down attitude in flight. Moving the cyclic stick aft causes the opposite movement, resulting in a nose-up attitude' (2-5-2).

The cyclic stick, being a convenient grip for the pilot, also features a range of other controls, including a cargo-hook release switch, a flare dispenser switch and, most prominently, a trim switch for the advanced flight control system (AFCS). (The HC-6 has the upgraded digital advanced flight control system/DAFCS from the F model as will the HC-4 and HC-5 in due course.) The AFCS is a computerised system for stabilising the helicopter, maintaining airspeed, altitude, bank angle and heading controls, and it is set on the canted console by the pilot's knees. While the AFCS is operating, the trim switch on the cyclic stick is used to make small changes in attitude. The cyclic also features a comms trigger, used when the pilot wants to talk to the rest of the crew. It provides a master override of the comms system. As one pilot clarified: 'If you need to talk to everyone on the crew – for example, you've just seen a missile launch – and everyone's talking, you just press that; it just blocks out everyone else but you.'

The final component in the flight controls are the yaw pedals. These alter the angle of the rotor discs to impart directional control during flight, but only below 40 knots. So, for example, to move to the right the pilot depresses the right pedal, which shifts the forward rotor disc to the right and the aft rotor disc to the left.

All the many control inputs are transmitted to the rotors through mechanical means to a mixing unit, which translates all the inputs into

LEFT The collective, also known as the 'thrust lever' by US forces, provides vertical lift. Raising the handle causes the pitch on all six rotor blades to increase, generating lift, while lowering the handle has the opposite effect. *(Author)*

BELOW A stand-alone example of the cyclic stick and the pilot's flight control pedals. The information from these controls goes into the mixing unit just aft of the cockpit, next to the forward transmission. *(Author)*

lateral cyclic- and collective-pitch motions. The mixing unit is a bewildering engineering masterpiece, rationalising the numerous mechanical instructions from the pilot into a few manageable instructions to the rotor system. Even engineers very familiar with the Chinook still remark that the complexity of the mixing unit defies easy description.

Instrument panels and avionics

Obviously it takes much more than two levers and two pedals to fly the Chinook. The pilots are surrounded by a total of six distinct instrument panels around the cockpit, each panel containing a variety of controls, gauges, switches and displays for everything from defensive aids to altimeters. The six instrument panels are as follows: pilot's instrument panel; co-pilot's instrument panel; centre instrument panel; canted console; centre console; and overhead console. The exact instruments contained on these panels changes to varying degrees between the marks (the cockpit levers and flying controls remain the same, however). In the earlier helicopters, for example, analogue controls dominated, while in the HC-4 a more streamlined digitised system is used, with flat-screen computer panels replacing entire banks of instruments.

In terms of the basic functions of the panels,

BELOW The pilot's seat in the HC-2 cockpit. The pilot's controls are repeated on the panel in front of the co-pilot. Note also the forward visibility down through the nose of the aircraft. *(Author)*

the pilot's and co-pilot's panels naturally contain flight-critical instrumentation, including torquemeter, airspeed indicator, attitude indicator, altimeter, vertical speed indicator, chronometer and rotor tachometer. Here a Chinook pilot explains the purpose of key instruments on these and other panels within the cockpit of a HC-2, and in so doing also details some of the key avionics installed into the Chinook:

'So, in the centre at the top [of the pilot's/ co-pilot's panels] you've got the AI, which is the attitude indicator, essentially your artificial horizon, and that tells you your angles of bank and nose-up and nose-down. So in cloud that would give you the horizon that you would normally see outside. To the right of that you have your radar altimeter – the rad alt – which is obviously very useful for low-level flying. It has alarms that you can set if you fly below a certain height. To the left you have the air-speed indicator (ASI), and below that you have the HSI [horizontal situation indicator], which is effectively your air compass. You also have a standby AI to the left of that, so if the main one fails you switch to the standby as backup. To the right you have your altimeter, which is your barometric altimeter. You have a clock – which is an important instrument – and to the other side of that you have your VSI [vertical speed indicator], which tells you how quickly you're going up and down. Right of the rad alt is your hover meter, and that can be used in a situation when you can't see outside and you're in a

hover. You can see a circle in the control; if you keep the cross over the centre of the circle this indicates that you're stable over one point.

'Your mode select panel is all to do with your

ABOVE **The pilot of this HC-4 Chinook reaches down to adjust the collective. Note how different types of information are displayed across the panels, according to pilot/co-pilot priorities.** *(Crown Copyright)*

navigation aids. So you've got UHF, VHF, FM Homer, your ILS [instrument landing system], the TACAN and ADF – these are all things really for instrument flying [flying based purely on information from the instruments, rather than external visual information]. For example, if you want to do an ILS approach you tune the ILS in on the ILS frequency, and then select the ILS button, and that will display the ILS information on the HSI and the AI. There's also your navigation panel and GPS panel. That set-up is repeated exactly the same over on the co-pilot's side.

'The cruise guide indicator effectively tells you how much stress is on the airframe – green is good, yellow indicates that you're starting to over-stress the aircraft and obviously red indicates that you can't do any more and the aircraft will require detailed checks by the engineers to ensure damage hasn't occurred. Below you have your torque meter – there's 100% at the top, but you can pull to 123% for a set period of time. And that is limited by altitude, so if you're hot-and-high [in hot weather at high altitudes] that 123% will come down. On a single engine you can pull to 150 if you need to, to make sure you get on the ground.

'Your rotor rpm indicator tells you how quickly your rotors are spinning. So at 100% the rotors are spinning at 225rpm. Generally you'll see your needle in the green, but when you go into autorotation [where the rotors are unpowered] you'll generally bring it into the yellow to give you that extra bit of inertia. The computer's engine management keeps it at 100% NR [N is speed and R refers to rotors, so NR = rotor blade speed in per cent of 225rpm] all the time when the engines are running. So the idea is that no matter what power you pull, which will change with weight, altitude and temperature, it will stay at 100%. If the NR starts to drop, you're out of power.

'All the instrumentation in the middle is your

engine instrumentation. You have your fire T-handles, so you pull those (in the unlikely event of an emergency, when alarms sound) to set off fire extinguishers in the engines. There is also an outside temperature gauge, which is quite important in the winter, because you don't want to be in cloud when it's freezing, as we have no icing protection on the blades.

'Then you have all your various different engine instruments – turbine speeds, turbine temperatures, oil temperatures etc. The transmission indications are kind of unique to the Chinook. Because we have so many gearboxes, you can't have all of the information relating to these displayed all of the time. So on 'scan' you get the oil pressure and oil temperature in the gearboxes, and it will display the lowest oil pressure and the highest oil temperature, so the system scans it for you and displays that information. Then every 15 minutes you undertake something called a 'scan check', so you switch between information on each of the gearboxes in turn and then go back to 'scan' to make sure that

it's functioning correctly. It has a green light in whichever one it's displaying. So if the left-hand transmission has the lower oil pressure, that will be displayed green. That's quite a good little system, because it scans everything for you – you wouldn't otherwise be able to get all that information up at the same time. With the HC-2 and HC-3, if we had the multi-function display here, however, we could display all of those values, all of the time.'

Given the huge array of systems in play in the Chinook, the crew naturally have to rely on automated means to alert them to potential problems. The cautionary advisory panel provides a centralised source for warnings, about everything from low oil pressure to electrical faults.

One useful avionics element in the Chinook is the doppler system, which is in effect a self-

ABOVE The pilot's controls on the left side of the Chinook. Note the flare release button on the cyclic stick, covered by the yellow-and-black patterned flip-up shield. The light is reflecting off the **CDNU.** *(Author)*

RIGHT An artificial horizon display in the cockpit. Such instruments are essential for 'instrument flying', when weather or dust conditions prevent the pilot from acquiring visual orientation. *(Author)*

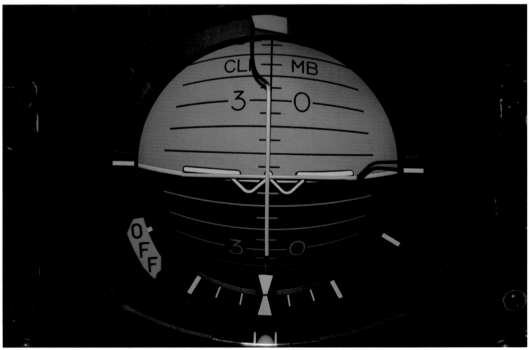

contained navigation system that doesn't rely on the presence of external navigation aids. A Chinook flight lieutenant explains its function: '[It] gives you your ground speed rather than your air speed. It also gives you your drift. So, for example, if we were in flight, it might show that you effectively need to offset by 5° to the left to stop yourself drifting. So it gives you your drift calculations.'

Looking upwards in the Chinook, the overhead console is less focused on advanced avionics systems but handles more basic engineering systems. It features engine, fuel and lighting management controls. The last includes troop warning lights, so that the pilot can illuminate green and red warning lights in the back, as the aforementioned flight lieutenant clarifies: 'If you're conducting a parachute deployment, for example, [you can use it] to indicate if you're approaching a landing site – red, approaching the site, green, time to get off.

There's an alarm by which you can ring a call bell, which we use when we start the aircraft and to get the attention of people.'

The canted console controls are focused more on operational and defensive functions rather than flight information. The control and display navigation unit (CDNU) sits to the left, and other elements of the canted console are the automatic flying control system (AFCS), longitudinal pitch indicator, a pilot's display control panel (on the HC-4) and the air-conditioning controls.

Lower down, the centre console gathers together much of the Chinook's communications and defensive controls. These include the controls for the AN/ALQ 156 and AN/ALQ 157

RIGHT The canted console on the HC-4. The display and keypad to the left relate to the CDNU, while in the centre (top to bottom) are the radar warning receiver, digital control display unit and successor identification friend or foe. On the right are the automatic flying control system, the pilot's display control panel, the air condition controls and the longitudinal pitch indicator. *(Crown Copyright)*

LEFT The Chinook's centre console contains a mass of kit, but is the main locus of the pilot's and co-pilot's communication systems and also the night-vision navigation tools. The switch at top left is for the engine air particle separator (EAPS). *(Crown Copyright)*

BELOW The overhead console serves many practical purposes, including control of the lighting, heating, ventilation, electricals, hydraulics, fuel and anti-icing systems. *(Crown Copyright)*

countermeasures suites, the TACAN (tactical air navigation) system, co-pilot's and pilot's communication control panels, dual Talon radios and the Bowman comms systems. In addition, the centre console features the grip control for the FLIR (forward-looking infrared unit, mounted beneath the helicopter's nose), night-vision display systems (NVG goggles and NVG searchlight) and the external antenna select switch.

Two of these systems are worth closer study. The AFCS is an automated system to help stabilise the aircraft in flight around all axes, and automatically maintaining desired airspeed, altitude, bank angle, and heading. A summary of its functions is as follows:

- Rate damping in all axes and sideslip stability.
- Pitch and roll attitude hold and heading hold.
- Airspeed hold.
- Improved control response in pitch, roll and yaw.
- Barometric and radar altitude hold.
- Automatic coupled turns.
- Longitudinal cyclic trim scheduling.

(Source ref: TM 1-1520-240-10, 2-5-7)

The AFCS dramatically improves the stability and performance of the Chinook in flight, while the CDNU is devoted to navigational priorities, as a Chinook pilot explains further: 'The CDNU is our navigation unit. In a civilian airliner this would be the pilot's flight planning or mission computer; basically this is the same thing, but obviously we use it for military functions. You can do all sorts with it. You can programme your routes into it, and it's a very clever piece of kit. The downside of the HC-2 and HC-3 is that you have no moving map; all your information is displayed as a trackbar [a bar that indicates whether the pilot is on the GPS track or drifting from it] and as data. It will give you information, such as you have 6.5 miles to your turning point, and you are 0.3 miles left of your track etc. You decide whatever you want it to display.' This situation has changed in the HC-4, which can now display moving maps to give the pilots a greater sense of operational awareness.

The defensive aids suite (DAS) refers to the fully automated systems the helicopter has to

protect itself from a range of threats, particularly from being targeted by radar-guided or heat-seeking surface-to-air missiles (SAMs). Much of this suite is contained on the canted console, including the radar warning receiver (RWR) and identification friend or foe (IFF) set. The RWR takes in information from multiple antennae situated on the outside of the Chinook, which respond to fire-control radars, providing an alert to the pilot when the helicopter is being 'acquired' by the enemy defences.

Communications

Being a four-person ship, and with the capacity to take many more people on board, the Chinook's internal communications have to be both flexible and reliable. An interphone network enables the crew to talk among themselves seamlessly. This has five stations around the helicopter – one each for the pilot and co-pilot, one at the forward end of the cabin for the troop commander, and two stations further back in the cabin for the loadmasters and weapon operators. There are also two external interphone reception panels.

BELOW A communications station for the crewman in the cabin. The Chinook has a comprehensive communications suite, for talking internally or externally via UHF, VHF, V/VHF, AM and FM networks. *(Author)*

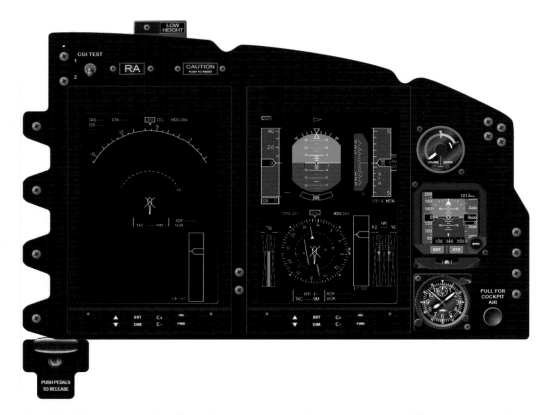

RIGHT The co-pilot's console on the HC-4. It is centred upon two multi-function display panels, to the right of which (top to bottom) are the cruise guide indicator, secondary flight display, standby slip/skid indicator, clock and (bottom right) cockpit air control. *(Crown Copyright)*

A 10m (33ft) interphone cable allows the crew members to move freely around the cabin, while remaining plugged into one of the stations.

For communications between helicopter and ground, multiple systems are used, the controls located on the centre console. A Chinook pilot explains: 'You have two Talon radios which have UHF-AM and VHF-AM on both, so you have quite a lot of communication options. Then you have a standby VHF box on its own, and a Bowman radio for talking to guys on the ground. You can select aerials, so you can have Talon B working on the upper aerial and Talon A working on the lower aerial, so if you have problems you

can flip between aerials.' There is also an HF radio for very long-range communications.

In the HC-2/2A the instrumentation described above was displayed in individual instruments, but times are changing with the HC-4 upgrade. In the HC-4 much of the information is shown via digital displays, particularly two large multi-function displays (MFDs) per pilot/co-pilot instrument panel, plus a standby flight display on the outboard of the panel, as part of the Thales TopDeck cockpit. A pilot might typically have flight information displayed on the outer MFD, while the inner MFD would contain navigation information or

RIGHT AND FAR RIGHT A manual flare release button, shown in both the open and closed positions. *(Author)*

START-UP PROCEDURE

The following is a standard start-up procedure for the Chinook; the quotes are explanations from an experienced Chinook flight lieutenant:

1 Arrive at the aircraft, and perform a walk-round check. Make sure that everything is in order, with no leaks or external damage. Turn on the external battery, 'so that when we walk on to the aircraft we can use its power'.

2 Once inside, use the external battery to provide basic functions, such as the ability to use the comms systems.

3 Do a series of checks to make sure that all switches are in the right position, and everything is off that should be, so the equipment doesn't experience an electrical spike when the power is turned on. Make sure all the emergency equipment is operable.

4 Start the APU. When the APU is up and running, the APU generator is turned on. 'That provides all the electrical power we need to get the aircraft up and running, and the APU also provides sufficient hydraulic power to start the engines.'

5 With power to the aircraft, all the cockpit switches are again checked to confirm they are in the right position. 'It's literally just a case of starting top left and working down one aisle and up the next.' During these checks, 'we have what's called engine condition levers (ECLs). There are two levers – one for the left engine and one for the right – and they're either at "stop", or in the middle position which is "ground", or the advanced position which is "flight". So we'll put them to "ground" at this stage and they basically provide information to the FADEC [full authority digital engine control]. So once they're at "ground" we're in a position to start that engine.' Other checks include an alarm test on the fire bottles in the engines, all the warning captions, all the flight instruments and the functionality of the auto-pilot. Hydraulics are tested: 'We'll isolate one system and make sure that one system can maintain the hydraulic functions by moving the [rotor] head, and we check the second system also.'

6 Following checks, the pilot can start the engine. The fuel pump is turned on, the ECLs are at 'ground' and the rotor brake is on, 'because although we want the engines to start we don't at this stage want the rotors to turn'. Then he operates the start switch and beins monitoring the engine instruments. 'What we're looking for when we operate the start switch is the N1 gauge; when that's above 12% we start to watch the PTIT, which is the turbine inlet temperature. We just monitor that to make sure that the engine is within the normal operating range, and the normal temperatures.' Once the engine is fully warmed up, the pilots release the rotor brake and the rotors start to turn. 'We go back to the ECL lever and advance it slowly to "flight", and what that does is get the blades up to full speed. So once it's up to flight the blades are turning at 100% of their revolutions per minute (225rpm).'

7 Once engines are running, the engine generators are turned on to provide power to the aircraft. Then the second engine is started, following the same procedure as described above. At flight, therefore, both of the ECLs will be at the 'flight' position.

8 Perform after-start checks – checks include fuel pressure, confirm that there are no DECU (digital electronic control unit) codes showing problems with the FADEC (rear crewmen check this).

9 Pre-taxi and final checks, then we are ready to get airborne.

ABOVE The centre instrument panel, containing various system displays, the emergency fire control and the caution/advisory panel, which displays problems in one colour-coded location. *(Crown Copyright)*

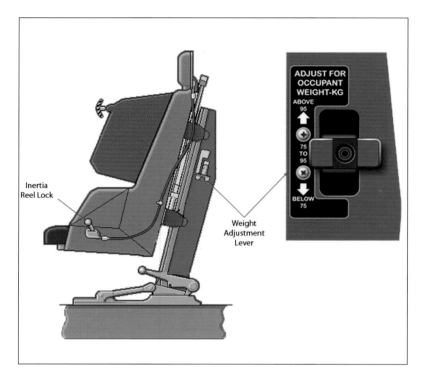

Inertia
Reel Lock

Weight
Adjustment
Lever

ADJUST FOR
OCCUPANT
WEIGHT-KG
ABOVE
95
↑
75
TO
95
↓
BELOW
75

ABOVE The aft flare release switch, placed so that a rear crewman on the ramp can have a defensive response to missile threats in his visual quadrant. *(Author)*

LEFT The Chinook's front seats are fully adjustable for weight and for posture. They also incorporate fixed and hinged armour panels to provide additional crew protection from small-arms fire. *(Crown Copyright)*

images displayed from the helicopter's FLIR system. The new system is specifically designed to reduce the pilot's workload under demanding operational conditions, and recent experience in Afghanistan has already proved its worth.

Fuselage

Flight Sergeant Mark Lilley, one of the senior engineers at Odiham, takes the simple view of the Chinook: 'You can describe the

RIGHT A view into the Chinook from the rear ramp. The handle on the forward right-hand side is a manual hand-pump for the hydraulic system. *(Author)*

Chinook as a flying three-ton truck. It's just a tube back there ... there's nothing complex about it, and that's the way it should be.' This statement certainly evokes the fundamental utility of the Chinook. The fact is that the bulk of the Chinook's body consists of empty space, in the form of a capacious cargo hold. Yet the simplicity is what gives the Chinook its incredible versatility in role performance.

Taking an external view, the Chinook's fuselage features two main points of entry and exit: the main cargo ramp at the rear and the starboard door just aft of the cockpit. The starboard door is structured in two sections: an upper jettisonable section, which swings up overhead on rails when opened normally, and a lower section that folds downwards to form a step. Note that the pilot and the co-pilot also have emergency cockpit doors, for rapid exit in emergency situations. Pulling or pushing the egress handles allows the whole door to be pushed outwards. In the cabin area, emergency egress is performed either via the starboard door or through the windows (five on each side of the fuselage) – a strap fitted to each window is pulled to break the window's seal, and the window can then be pushed out. The port front window has a larger jettisonable frame than the other windows. An emergency escape hatch is

also fitted to the main ramp, and a further hatch is located at the midpoint in the cargo hold floor, beneath the utility-hatch door.

Inside the cargo hold, the cargo floor is

BELOW The port window panel. Like all the Chinook's windows, this one can be jettisoned in an emergency, by breaking a seal that holds it to the fuselage. *(Crown Copyright)*

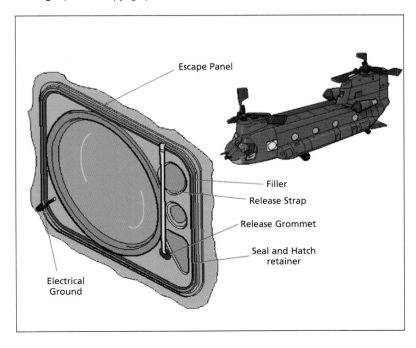

Escape Panel

Filler

Release Strap

Release Grommet

Seal and Hatch retainer

Electrical Ground

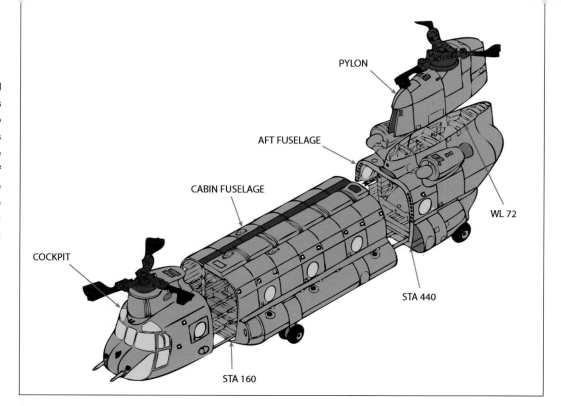

PYLON

AFT FUSELAGE

CABIN FUSELAGE

COCKPIT

WL 72

STA 440

STA 160

made from extruded panels, riveted together in sections, with rollered sections running the length of the floor to provide lower-friction surfaces for moving cargo along the hold. The flooring either side of the centreline is also strengthened to take the weight of tracks or wheels, when the Chinook is transporting vehicles. Rubber vibration isolators set beneath

key sections of the flooring reduce internal load vibrations.

For securing cargo to the floor space, 83 tie-down ring fittings are provided at regularly spaced intervals, each fitting capable of taking a 5,000lb (2,272kg) load, with an additional eight 10,000lb (4,545kg) fittings along the outer edge of the cabin. There are also studs for fitting

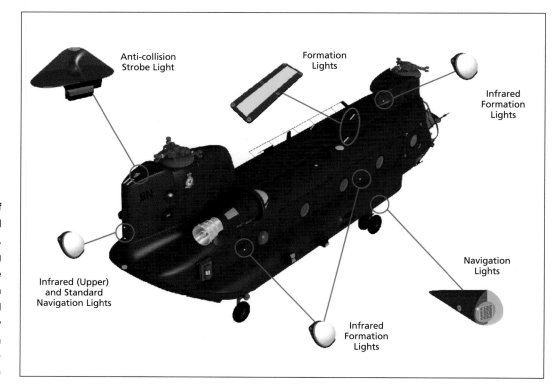

Anti-collision Strobe Light

Formation Lights

Infrared Formation Lights

Navigation Lights

Infrared (Upper) and Standard Navigation Lights

Infrared Formation Lights

equipment such as troop seats and medical litters. Here is the real beauty of the Chinook. The internal configurations are highly variable according to the tactical demands. In terms of the troop transportation, for example, 33 seats in total are normally fitted into the cabin area – 16 starboard and 17 port. However, if additional seating is required another 11 rearward-facing seats can be installed along the centre of the cabin. A folding troop commander's seat is located in the cockpit doorway. For casualty-recovery missions, the cabin can be fitted with up to 23 stretchers, in five tiers of four and one of three, using litter poles and webbing straps. Other configurations of the cabin include static-line parachuting and fast-rope/abseiling (here

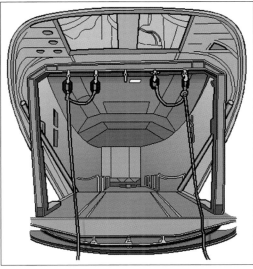

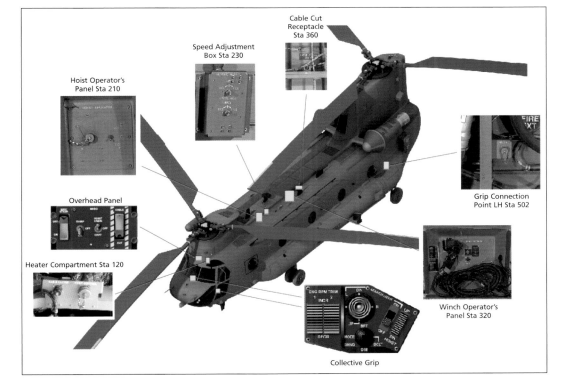

Cable Cut Receptacle Sta 360

Speed Adjustment Box Sta 230

Hoist Operator's Panel Sta 210

Overhead Panel

Heater Compartment Sta 120

Grip Connection Point LH Sta 502

ENG RPM TRIM

Winch Operator's Panel Sta 320

Collective Grip

an RFRF – rear fast-roping frame – is fitted to the upper edge of the rear door frame). A water dam can even be fitted internally which enables the Chinook to land into water with its rear cargo door open. This fitment, used for amphibious deployment or recovery of troops and equipment, allows the water to flood into the rear cabin without flowing forward into the front cabin and cockpit areas.

The HC-4 now also has a multi-function operator's seat (MFOS) and pallet assembly in the cabin. The RAF's 'A tech M Course' manual describes the MFOS and pallet assembly as giving 'a safe and crashworthy working environment in the forward cabin area. A pallet is used to attach the MFOS to the helicopter floor. The pallet helps the crewmember use the heater instrumentation panel and weapon system offering several seat positions between the left cabin emergency escape panel and the right cargo compartment door. Multiple seat adjustments can be made for crewmember comfort. The MFOS has a four-point harness system with reels that lets the crewmember stand up with the harness.'

Features such as the MFOS reflect the need to reduce physical fatigue in crewmembers, as traditionally the Chinook can be physically wearing to those who have to spend many hours inside. For this reason, the Chinook is also fitted with an anti-vibration system, here explained by Flight Sergeant Lilley: 'The self-tuning vibration absorber (STVA) basically senses the vibrations of the aircraft, and it makes this huge block of concrete vibrate in such a way as to cancel out the vibrations from the airframe, very similar to the block of concrete in a washing machine. There's one under each pilot and it takes a lot of the fatigue out of flying the Chinook. There's also another one in the nose which goes towards stopping the vibrations in the panels.' The US Army's Chinook manual expands on the technicalities of the system: 'The self-tuning feature of the dynamic absorber functions as follows: each dynamic absorber consists of a tuning mass suspended by springs, and electronic measuring circuit, accelerometers, counterweights, an electrical actuator and a self test box. The accelerometers sense and compare the vibration phases of the helicopter and the spring mounted mass.

When the measured vibration phases differ from a built-in phase relationship required to assure proper tune, the electronic circuit extends or retracts the electrical actuator to reposition the counterweights which, in turn, increases or decreases the resonant frequency of the spring-mounted mass. The dynamic absorbers are constantly being adjusted (tuned) to minimise helicopter vibration' (TM 1-1520-240-10, 2.1.22).

To improve the protection offered to the Chinook's occupants, the cabin can be fitted with ballistic panels, again explained by Flight Sergeant Lilley: 'The ballistic panels come to about halfway up the windows when they're fitted to create an armoured "bathtub". So when the guys are sitting down the panels protect them to about head height. Additionally there's extra protection from fuel spraying and igniting into the cabin from a damaged fuel tank from a projectile. The cabin area walls have a Kevlar and Atamel meld blanket fitted. The Kevlar stops or slows down projectiles from penetrating, while the Atamel absorbs any fuel that's sprayed in and pushes it down to the floor. So this is just one more level of protection for troops and crew using the Chinook.'

In terms of other equipment to facilitate cabin operations, there is a 3,000lb (1,364kg) hydraulically operated winch mounted at right forward of the cabin, and used for pulling loads into the cargo hold with 150ft (46m) of usable cable. With the aid of pulley blocks, it is capable of drawing 12,000lb (5,454kg) of equipment, whereas in a straightforward hoisting mode the strain is reduced to 600lb (272kg). The winch can operate at two speeds – 20fpm (cargo loading) and 100fpm (hoisting). The cable drum is automatically locked when the power supply is off, and the winch is also equipped with an automatic stop should the strain exceed 3,200lb (1,454kg).

The winch is controlled either from the cockpit or by a loadmaster in the cabin. Note, however, that the cockpit controls override those used in the cabin, so the pilots can manage the needs of both loading and flight safety. When the winch is controlled from the cabin, the loadmaster does so by means of a pistol-shaped grip, which features switches for hoisting, winching and cargo-hook operations, plus a comms switch. In cases where a hoisted load needs to be jettisoned immediately, the

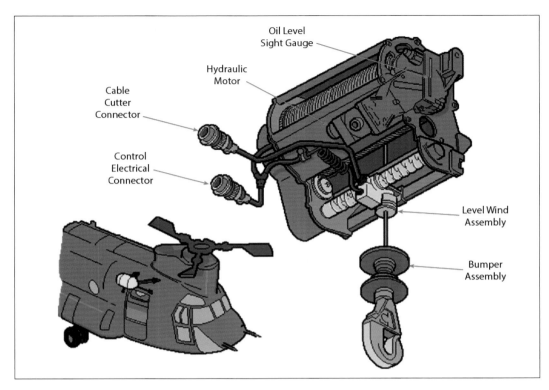

Cable
Cutter
Connector

Control
Electrical
Connector

Oil Level
Sight Gauge

Hydraulic
Motor

Level Wind
Assembly

Bumper
Assembly

LEFT The Chinook's external hoist, fitted above the starboard front door, used for light personnel and cargo lifting. *(Crown Copyright)*

BELOW The locations and primary controls for the Chinook's fore, centre and aft hooks. In the top right of this diagram is the portable pistol-shaped winch/hoist control grip, which can be plugged in stations either side of the cabin. *(Crown Copyright)*

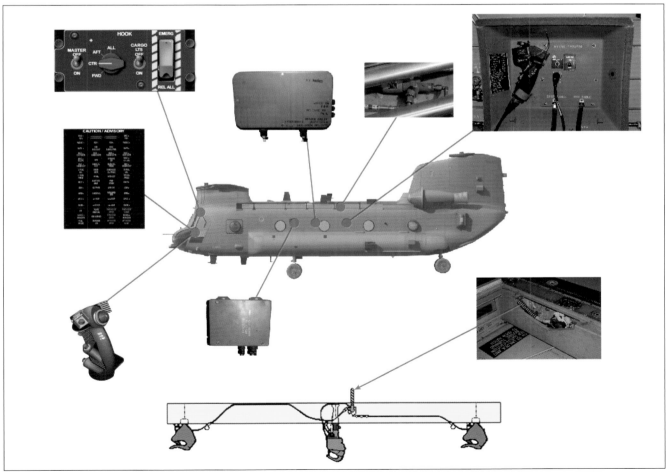

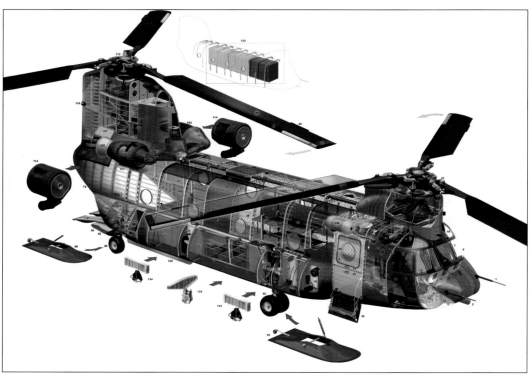

RIGHT Chinook general cutaway. *(Courtesy Boeing)*

BELOW An exploded view of the front landing gear, which are of fixed cantilever type. Each landing gear is fitted with an individual air-oil shock strut. *(Crown Copyright)*

loadmaster can operate a cable-cutter system. Pressing the cable-cutter button initiates an electrical circuit that in turn fires a ballistic cable-cutting cartridge, giving instant ejection of the winched load.

Loading ramp

The cargo ramp, set behind the main rear cabin door, is the central loading bay for the Chinook. It can also be used to support portions of the helicopter's load that don't actually fit inside the main cabin (the ramp has to be aligned with the cabin floor for this function), although the weight of the cargo on the ramp portion must not exceed 3,000lb (1,364kg). There are two portions to the ramp: the main portion, hinged directly to the airframe, and three auxiliary ramp extensions. The ramp extensions are used to provide a flush contact between the ground and the ramp, thereby enabling vehicles to drive straight into the cabin. (The central ramp extension also serves as an APU work platform.) The lateral position of the ramp extensions can be adjusted to accommodate vehicles or different wheelbases, and when not in use they can either be removed or are stored in an inverted position against the ramp. In combat operations, the ramp can also be used to mount an M60 machine gun, for rearward defence.

Landing gear

There are four non-retractable landing gears on a Chinook, located in pods beneath the fuselage. The forward landing gear consists of dual-wheel assemblies of a fixed-cantilever type, while the after assemblies are single wheels that

Cylinder Assembly

Plugs

Tie-Down Lug

Torque Arm

Brake Assembly

Axle

FUEL TANKS AND THE FARE SYSTEM

Total fuel capacity for the Chinook HC-2/4/6 at standard range is 3,910 litres (860.3 gallons), set in six tanks (main, forward and aft aux, port and starboard) running along the lower edges of the airframe. To increase the range of the Chinook dramatically, Sergeant John Chadwick explains that 'the Chinook can also fit three extended range fuel tanks (ERT) on the inside, in the cabin. Each of those tanks holds about 2.4 tons of fuel. That will obviously provide the aircraft itself with a massively extended range. What we can also do is attach a FARE [forward air refuelling equipment] kit, which is essentially a stand-alone-pump. We can take the fuel out of those ERTs, and then use the Chinook as a refuelling station for smaller aircraft, or another Chinook, on the ground.' The FARE unit, which sits in the cargo area aft of the ERTs, can be set up in about 20 minutes, the flow of fuel to multiple nozzles (up to 60m/200ft away from the main aircraft) controlled by a simple operator's handgrip. The system is so simple to use that one man alone can operate it.

Naturally, the fuel system presents safety concerns, so the Chinook has various protective measures to guard against fire. Flight Sergeant Lilley: 'We've got fire extinguisher systems for the engines, and engine bays, and we've got hand-held fire extinguishers dotted all over the place, but the Chinook tends not to catch fire. We've got a COBRA system [an automatic fire-suppression system] which will suppress fire on the outside of the fuel tanks;

the fuel tanks are also self-sealing, and they'll take up to a .50-calibre round. The tanks being on the outside of the aircraft and not internal to the aircraft is another safety feature. We've got frangible couplings on the fuel system designed to sheer or break when they encounter heavy G-loads and impacts [such as during a crash], which means that the fuel tanks separate from the aircraft. All the electrical connections are spring-loaded bayonet connections, and they're strapped to the airframe. So if for any reason your fuel tank pulls away, all it will do is safely disconnect the connections, rather than having wires flapping around.'

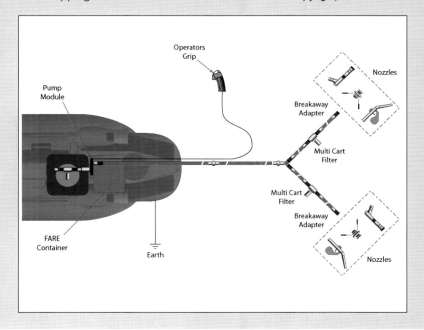

have full-swivel (360° turn), but which can be power-centred and locked.

Each individual landing gear is fitted with an individual air-oil shock strut, and the two aft wheels also feature landing gear proximity switches, explained by the US CH-47D manual thus: 'Each switch is activated when its associated shock strut is compressed during touchdown. The switches improve ground handling by reducing pitch axis gain of the AFCS, by canceling the longitudinal Control Position Transducer (CPT), therefore longitudinal stick input, to the Differential Airspeed Hold (DASH) actuators, and by driving both

Longitudinal Cyclic Trim (LCT) actuators to the ground position.'

The Chinook's capability to operate in all manner of terrain and climate means that it must also be capable of landings into snow. For this reason, ski fittings are available for mounting on all the landing gear.

As we have seen, the Chinook is a compelling engineering package. Supporting its prodigious lift and utility capabilities is a design with redundancy and duplicated systems built in as standard, to give the aircraft the reliability that keeps it operational many decades after its design was originally conceived.

Chapter Three

Engine power – Honeywell T55-L-714A

The beating heart of the Chinook has been the T55 generation of turboshaft engines. Designed by the Lycoming company in the 1950s, the T55 has proven itself time and time again under a testing range of climatic and environmental conditions, from the jungles of Vietnam to the arctic wastes of Scandinavia. Through a constant programme of upgrades, the engine series has managed to stay utterly relevant to operational conditions, delivering the power and the reliability required of combatant nations the world over.

OPPOSITE The port 714A engine. Note the shaft running out from the front of the engine, which takes the power from the engine into the combining transmission. *(Author)*

The T55 evolution

The earliest American CH-47A Chinooks were fitted with Lycoming T55-L-5 power plants, which had a combined power output of 2,200shp. Yet such was just the beginning of a long evolution of the Chinook power plant. The power output was quickly extended by the T55-L-7, rated at 2,650shp or T55-L-7C engines rated at 2,850shp, the latter going into the CH-47B.

As Chapter 1 explains, with the evolution of the CH-47B into the CH-47C the Chinook moved over into RAF use. In the aircraft's HC-1 format, the first engines were Lycoming T55-L-11E turboshafts. Eight of the HC-1s delivered between 1984 and 1986 used the Lycoming T55-L-712 engines of the CH-47D.

With the development of the HC-2 came the Textron Lycoming T55-L-712F standard (Textron purchased Lycoming in 1986). The power output of each engine was 3,148shp, and the T55-L-712F became the cornerstone of the HC-2/HC-2A helicopters. It also featured full authority digital engine controls (FADEC), an automated system for controlling the engine operating parameters. For a time, controversy dogged FADEC, which was blamed by some for the hideous Chinook crash on the Mull of Kintyre, Scotland, on 2 June 1994, which killed 29 passengers and the 4 crew. Concerns among crews and engineers about FADEC continued for some time, but it has gone on to become a dependable and appreciated part of the aircraft.

In 1994, Textron sold its Turbine Engine Division, which, through a complex series of mergers and acquisitions, became part of Honeywell Aerospace in 1999. In 2009 the Ministry of Defence approved Honeywell's supply of T55-L-714A engines and spares for the RAF Chinook fleet, the power plants being upgraded in existing airframes from 2010.

The characteristics of the T55-L-714A show how far the engine has come since the early days of the CH-47A. In its current incarnation it delivers a maximum of 5,069shp, providing 20% more payload capability in hot-and-high conditions via a 22% increase in power output when compared to the previous engines. It also offers 7% lower fuel consumption and a time between overhauls of 3,000 hours (previously 2,400 hours), plus a greater durability of parts. This engine will provide the RAF's Chinook fleet with power for the foreseeable future, extending the life of these already venerable aircraft even further.

Engine structure and function

The T55 gas turbine engine can be divided into three major sections, from front to back: a compressor section, a combustor section, and the turbine section that delivers the power generated by the engine to the transmissions and ultimately to the rotors.

When the engine begins to operate, the compressor section, consisting of seven compressor stages and a centrifugal impeller all mounted on a common shaft, is turned by the starter system, the power initially provided by the APU. Air is drawn into the compressor section, where it is compressed by the compressor rotor blades and flowed through the air diffuser and into the combustion chamber. Some of the air is mixed with fuel, injected from two starting nozzles. The combustible air/fuel mix is ignited by four spark igniters, and the expanding gases

BELOW Two gas turbine engines like the one shown here provide the main power for the Chinook; the fourth turbine disc is viible at the left of the picture. *(Author)*

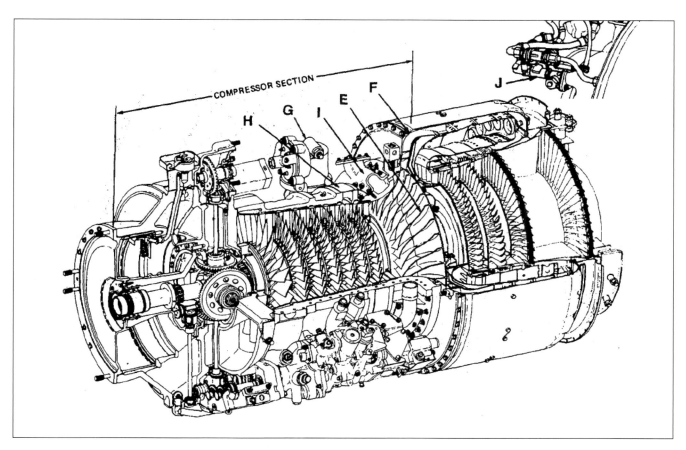

thus produced are pushed through the engine's turbine section. Some of the power provided by these gases drives two gas producer turbine discs, which in turn drive the compressor rotor, while the remainder of the energy drives two power turbine discs that propel the output shaft. The engine is driven up to a certain speed, at which point the hydromechanical assembly (HMA) and flow divider allow main fuel to flow to 28 main fuel nozzles. The fuel flows into the combustion chamber where it is ignited by burning starting fuel, increasing the power delivered to the power turbine discs.

The efficient functioning of the engine during this entire process is handled by the engine control system, which consists of several elements, including the compressor bleed control, turbine temperature control, torque sensing system and overspeed controls. The FADEC system, as denoted by Honeywell in their publicity, is essentially there to ease pilot workload and to provide diagnostics. Part of the FADEC, the digital electronic control unit (DECU), is mounted within the cabin and contains primary and backup controls,

plus a diagnostic fault display window and a serial data port for downloading data on engine performance. The integrated HMA is mounted on the engine accessory gearbox, and features a jet-induced high-pressure fuel pump, an integral alternator and a separate electromechanical primary fuel metering unit and backup reversionary fuel control.

Compressor unit

In total the 714A engine measures 47in (1,196mm), and two-thirds of this length is taken up by the compressor unit at the front. As suggested by the description above, the core functions of the compressor unit are to control the flow of air into the engine and that air's compression and distribution internally. Other functions include air cooling for internal parts of the engine and seal pressurisation.

Air first enters the compressor unit through the air inlet housing assembly, which also includes an ambient air temperature sensor. The air follows the path provided by the compressor housing, which gradually reduces

ABOVE Compressor section: E) centrifugal impeller; F) air diffuser; G) interstage air-bleed actuator; H) compressor bleed band; I) air gallery cover; J) water wash system. *(US Army)*

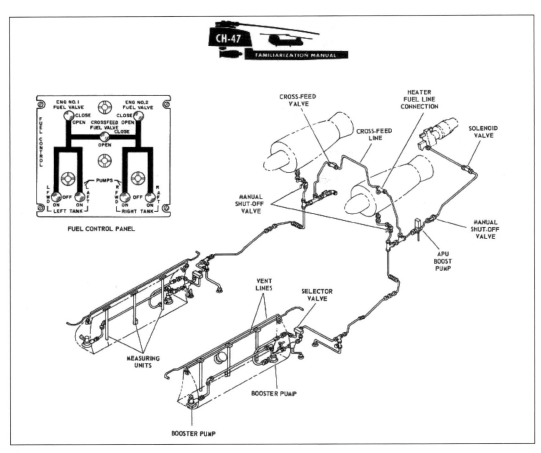

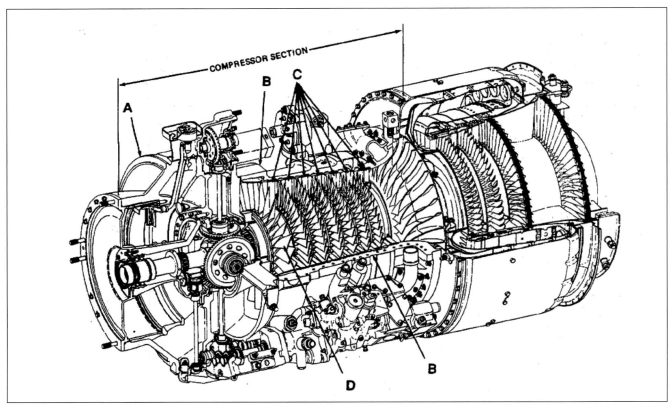

in diameter from front to back to initiate the air compression. Attached to the inside of the compressor housing are stator vanes, which control the directional flow of the air so that it hits the compressor vanes at the optimum angle for efficient operation.

In quick succession, the air now passes through seven rotating compressor stages in rapid succession. Each of the compressor rotor stages raises the air pressure, and a centrifugal impeller – itself an integral part of the compressor rotor assembly – compresses the air further and directs it through an air diffuser, which is responsible for directing the flow of the air between the centrifugal impeller and the combustion chamber. The air diffuser also includes vanes that remove some of the air swirl created by the centrifugal impeller. During this stage a pneumatic interstage air-bleed actuator controls air bleed by tightening or loosening a compressor bleed band around vent holes toward the rear of the compressor housing. This feature allows the helicopter to accelerate without a problematic surge of power caused by differing efficiencies of the axial compressor assembly and the centrifugal impeller compressor.

Combustion section

The combustion section makes up much of the remainder of the engine length, and it attaches directly to the air diffuser assembly. Functions of this section are primarily to give the engine an area for combustion and gas expansion. The outer wall of the chamber is formed by the combustion chamber housing, a structural component that includes mounting surfaces for main fuel manifold, fireshield, flow divider, spark igniters and start fuel nozzles. Also mounted to the combustion chamber housing are vanes that, along with those in the air diffuser, reduce air swirl and distribute the air consistently within the combustion section. Inside the combustion chamber housing is the combustion chamber lining, through which controlled amounts of air and fuel are allowed for combustion. At the bottom of the chamber housing, however, are two drain valve assemblies. These work to allow unburnt fuel to drain away when the engine is not running. Each valve assembly is a spring-loaded unit that is held closed by engine air pressure when the engine is running, but springs open when

BELOW The combustion section of the 714 engine: A) combustion chamber housing; B) combustion chamber liner; C) combustion chamber vanes; D) drain valve assembly. *(US Army)*

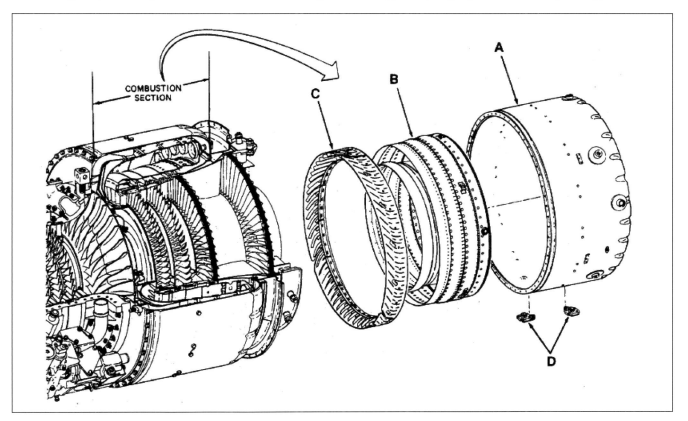

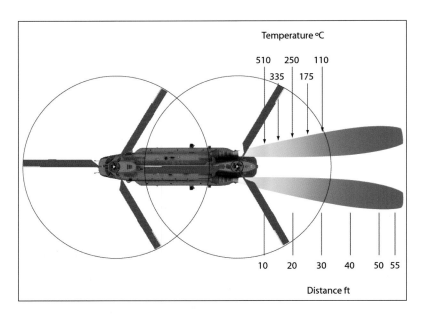

LEFT A diagram showing the temperatures of the gases exhausted from the Chinook's engines, and how the temperature diminishes over distance. *(Crown Copyright)*

the engine has stopped. The expanded hot gases then flow through an Yttrium stabilised zirconium curl, changing the direction of the hot gases by 180° leading into the turbine section.

Turbine section

The purpose of the turbine section is simple – it takes the energy created by the combustion process and turns it into usable power to drive the helicopter's rotors. It includes both gas producer and power turbine components.

Directly behind the air diffuser sits the curl assembly. Its purpose is to create an outer wall for the flow of hot gases being generated by combustion. Like the air diffuser, the curl assembly gives the turbulent gas flow a more orderly direction, and channels the flow towards the first gas producer nozzle. This nozzle is located forward of the first gas producer disc assembly. Again, like the curl assembly, the outer wall of the first gas producer nozzle forms a channel for the hot combustion gases, and nozzle vanes direct the gas so that they hit the first gas producer disc blades – set aft of the nozzle – efficiently. This arrangement of gas producer nozzle and gas producer disc assembly is then repeated in quick succession. Note that the gas producer disc assemblies are coupled directly to the compressor rotor assembly, so that as the hot gases strike the disc assembly blades the blades turn, which also causes the compressor rotor to turn.

The power turbine assembly section of the 714A, moving further towards the rear of the engine, features two further disc assemblies and two corresponding nozzles. The power shaft and third turbine disc (or the first power turbine

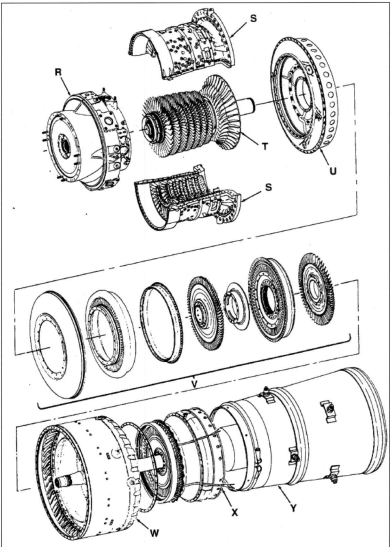

LEFT Exploded view of the Textron Lycoming 714: R) air inlet housing assembly; S) compressor housing assembly; T) compressor rotor assembly; U) air diffuser assembly; V) gas producer turbine section; W) combuster assembly; X) power turbine assembly; Y) tailpipe assembly. *(US Army)*

RIGHT The Chinook's auxiliary power unit (APU). Although small in size, the APU produces enough volume to inflict permanent hearing damage if crew stand close without ear protection. *(Author)*

disc) and the fourth turbine disc assembly (or second power turbine disc) are mounted together on an integral shaft assembly to form a single unit. The hot gases, channelled by the turbine nozzles, turn the whole integral shaft assembly. Here is the moment when the power of the engine is converted into a workable force for the rotors. The integral shaft assembly is splined to the output shaft in front of the engine, so when the assembly turns the output shaft turns also at a constant 16,000rpm. A bearing package, containing twin bearings, is mounted in the fourth turbine nozzle, supporting the rear of the integral shaft assembly between the third and fourth turbine discs. At the front of the power turbine section are also five thermocouple harness assemblies, each with two probes: 'Ten probe ends insert into and mount around third turbine nozzle and support. Leads fit through five guide tubes located

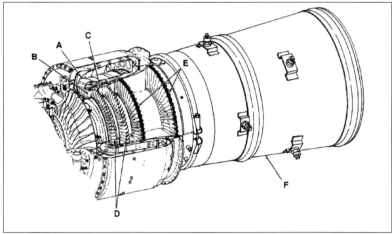

RIGHT The T55 714 turbine section: A) curl assembly; B) first gas producer nozzle; C) second gas producer nozzle; D) gas producer disk assemblies; E) power turbine assembly; F) tailpipe assembly. *(US Army)*

LEFT A detailed cutaway of the Honeywell 714A engine, clearly showing the number of bladed fans used to process the air and air/fuel passage through the engine. *(Honeywell)*

RIGHT This diagram illustrates the airflow through the Chinook's engine. Note how nearly two-thirds of the engine length is given to air intake and compression. *(Crown Copyright)*

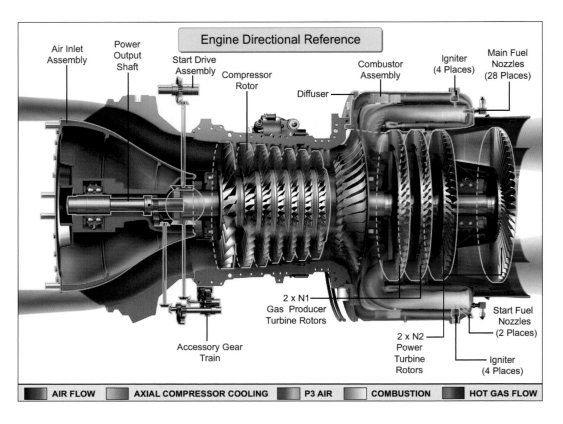

Engine Directional Reference

Air Inlet Assembly — Power Output Shaft — Start Drive Assembly — Compressor Rotor — Diffuser — Combustor Assembly — Igniter (4 Places) — Main Fuel Nozzles (28 Places)

2 x N1 Gas Producer Turbine Rotors — Accessory Gear Train — 2 x N2 Power Turbine Rotors — Start Fuel Nozzles (2 Places) — Igniter (4 Places)

AIR FLOW | AXIAL COMPRESSOR COOLING | P3 AIR | COMBUSTION | HOT GAS FLOW

around fourth turbine nozzle and secure to bus bar assembly. Probes made of materials which when heated react by developing a proportional voltage. The average of these voltages is reflected by cockpit indicator calibrated to read temperature in degrees centigrade' (TM1-2840-252-1, 1.23).

The rearmost component of the 714 engine is the tailpipe assembly. At its simplest, this is just a system for venting the hot exhaust gases into the external world. It works to reduce the gas temperatures as much as possible before they are released outward, but for those people outside, the exhaust still needs to be treated with respect. With the engines running at full power the temperature of the exhaust gases is 510°C (950°F) at 3m (10ft) from the tailpipe, 250°C (482°F) at 6.4m (20ft) and 110°C (230°F) at 9m (30ft). The velocity of the gases naturally diminishes over distance. At just 3m (10ft) from exit, they have a velocity of 63m/sec (207ft/sec), dropping to 25m/sec (82ft/sec) at 6m (20ft) and 13m/sec (43ft/sec) at 8.5m (28ft). The tailpipe is angled to direct the hot gases 8° up and 8° outboard to prevent heat damage to the airframe.

BELOW A cross-section of the Chinook's power plant. At its simplest, the engine works by taking in air, compressing it and mixing it with fuel, igniting the mix and using the resulting power to drive the turbines. *(Crown Copyright)*

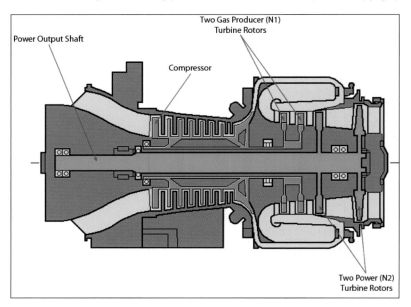

Power Output Shaft — Compressor — Two Gas Producer (N1) Turbine Rotors — Two Power (N2) Turbine Rotors

OPPOSITE The Textron Lycoming 714 engine, indicating: A) starter drive assembly; b) main fuel filter; C) starting fuel solenoid valve; E) pressurising valve and flow divided; and F) FADEC system. *(US Army)*

ENGINE AIR PARTICLE SEPARATOR (EAPS)

Modern aviation engines are greedy devices, sucking in huge volumes of air to feed the process of combustion. Being a battlefield helicopter, however, means that the Chinook's engines also take in all the detritus mixed with the air, including grit, sand, pieces of foliage, snow and ice and salt spray. Naturally, the foreign bodies are wearing on precision engine parts, and for this reason the Chinook's engines can be fitted with the engine air particle separator system (EAPS). (Note that some modern manufacturers expand the EAPS acronym as 'engine advanced protection system'.)

EAPS is effectively a giant self-cleaning filter system fitted over the air intake of the engine, and designed to trap and exhaust foreign bodies before they can reach the compressor section. EAPS is only fitted when required and is mounted on rails to the front of the engine, and can be removed easily by the engineers for engine inspections. It consists of 3,180 vortex tubes, the air flowing into the tubes being given a swirling motion by a fixed-blade fan.

As the contaminated air swirls ever more quickly through the EAPS, centrifugal force is imparted to the foreign bodies, throwing them outwards, where they are collected and ducted away before they enter the compressor section. Note that because the flow of the air itself continues centrally down the EAPS tube, there is no drop in the air pressure delivered to the compressor.

Should the EAPS experience a blockage, the system is fitted with bypass doors that enable the engine to keep running even with its EAPS out of action. The bypass doors are mounted flush with the front of the outer surface of EAPS, and are opened by electronic actuators by the pilot. With these doors opened, the air inflow is redirected around the separator inlet, straight to the compressor section of the engine. However, Chinook manuals caution against opening the bypass doors in snowy or icy conditions, the result of which can be injected snow and ice directly into the engine itself, with potentially catastrophic effects.

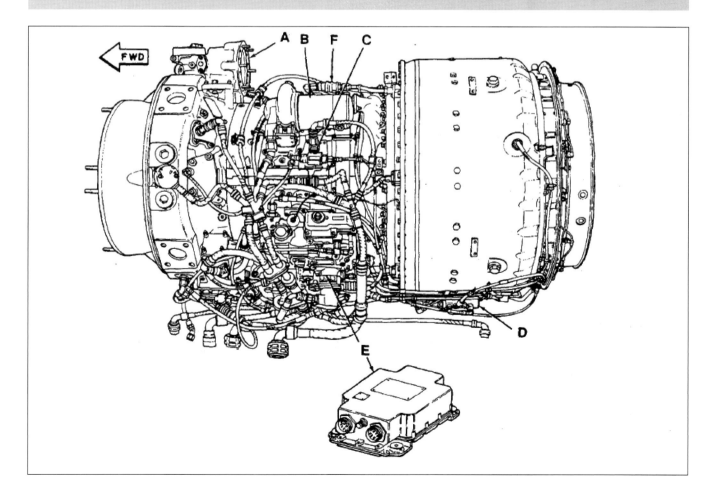

Transcmissions

For the rotors to turn, power is generated by the twin engines and that power is translated into rotating force via a powertrain system. Each engine has its own transmission, set at the forward edge of the engine. The engine's power is transferred out via a quill shaft that drives the spiral bevel pinion gear, which in turn drives the spiral bevel gear and shaft assembly, at which point the direction of torque is changed through 90°, reducing speed by 1.23 to 1. The torque is then directed through a one-way drive sprag clutch to the output shaft, then from the engine transmissions to the combining transmission.

The combining transmission, as its name suggests, has the role of taking the force supplied by the engines and supplying it in a coordinated fashion to the fore and aft transmissions. In doing so, the combining transmission also reduces the shaft speed to manageable levels. An early US CH-47 explains how the combining transmission combines the torque from both engines:

'The torque from both engines is combined within the transmission by means of two spiral bevel input pinion gears and a single spiral bevel ring gear. The spiral bevel input pinion gears receive the torque from the engine transmissions and both gears drive the ring gear. A speed reduction of 1.77 to 1 occurs at this point. The transmittal of longitudinal torque is accomplished by forward and aft output shafts; the ring gear is bolted to the aft shaft.' (CH-47 Familiarisation Manual, p.29.)

The combining transmission, given its utterly central role in the flight of the aircraft, is actually surprisingly small. Also of some surprise is the diameter of the aluminium synchronising shafts that run out from the combining transmission to the fore and aft transmissions. Failure of these components is extremely rare, despite the stresses under which they are placed. David McMullon, author of *Chinook: The Special Forces Flight in War and Peace*, notes of these components: 'Although the synchronising shafts look incredibly flimsy they're not. I've never heard of one breaking. Problems are usually caused by the thrust bearings in the gearbox. There are large splines in the gearbox and the ends of the shafts also have splines so they can slot in together. In one case I witnessed at Odiham the female end of the spline had not been fitted correctly. It engaged but not fully. On the ground everything was fine but once you lifted under power there was a lot of strain on the spline because it hadn't fully engaged. So

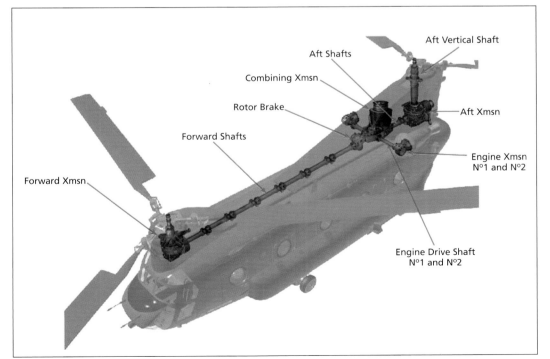

OPPOSITE This image clearly shows how the engine power is transferred via shafts into the combining transmission (in the centre of the photograph), then channelled out via the synchronising shaft. *(Author)*

LEFT An excellent view of the Chinook's powertrain, showing how the power from the engine meets in the combining transmission and is then diverted along forward and aft shafts to the rotors. *(Crown Copyright)*

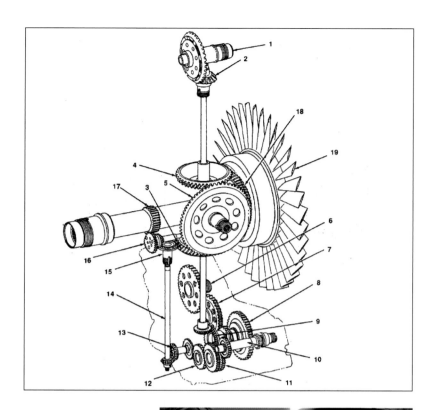

ABOVE A diagram of the 714 engine geartrain subsystem. Key parts in the diagram are: 1) gearshaft assembly; 5) bevel gear; 17) output shaft; and 19) compressor rotor assembly. *(US Army)*

CENTRE A view of the transmission shaft housing through the transmission tunnel access door, running along the back of the Chinook. *(Author)*

RIGHT The T55 714 shaft assembly: G) third turbine nozzle and support; H) integral shaft assembly; I) fourth turbine nozzle; J) Nos 4 and 5 bearing package; K) fourth turbine disc assembly; L) thermocouple harness assembly. *(US Army)*

it sheared off. This immediately desynchronised the rotor blades, which promptly hit each other.' Thankfully, such catastrophic incidents are extremely rare, and both synchronising shafts and transmissions are known for their reliability.

Once the power enters the forward and aft transmissions, it is then redirected to supply the horizontal turning force for the rotors. The forward and aft transmissions take the torque from the combining transmission and apply it to turning the rotors. Within the transmissions, a spiral bevel input pinion ring meshes with a spiral bevel ring gear, at which point the torque is redirected from the horizontal to the vertical plane, 9° tilted forward for the forward transmission output shaft and 4° tilted forward for the aft transmission output to the AVS shaft, running up to the rotors. The manual previously quoted here explains the complex gearing that takes place during this process:

'The ring gear is bolted to the first stage sun gear. The sun gear, in turn, drives the first stage planet gears which mesh with a stationary ring gear. The non-rotating ring gear causes the planet gears to revolve around the sun gear. The planet gears are attached to the first stage carrier which also revolves around the sun gear. The upper portion of the first stage carrier forms the second stage sun gear and it drives the second stage planet gears. These planet gears are attached to a second stage carrier and revolve in the same manner as the first stage planet gears and carrier. ... In the forward transmission, the second

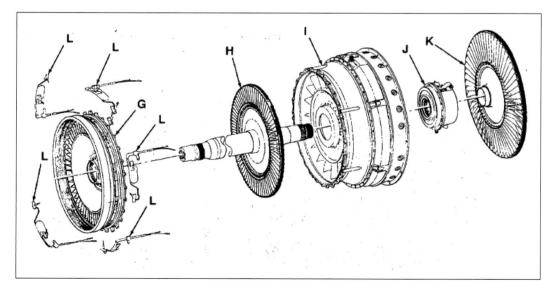

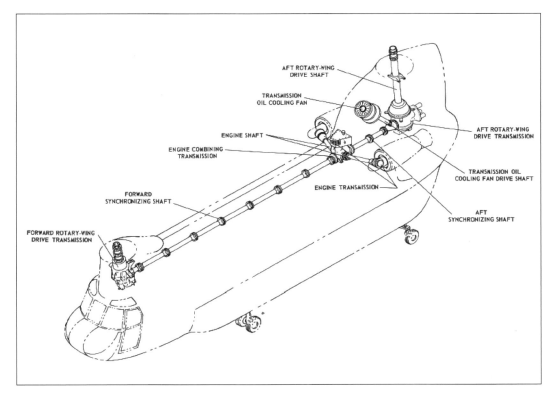

LEFT Another view of the Chinook power-train, this time from a 1960s US manual. The synchronising shaft itself is about the same thickness as a pencil, despite the role it performs. *(US Army)*

stage carrier is bolted to the rotor shaft; in the aft transmission, the second stage carrier is splined to receive the aft rotary-wing driveshaft [which in RAF nomenclature is called the aft vertical shaft]. The forward transmission rotor shaft is splined to receive the forward rotary-wing head. The aft rotary-wing (vertical) shaft is splined to receive the aft rotary-wing head.' (CH-47 Familiarisation Manual, p.31.)

Note that the combining forward and aft transmissions each have independent main and auxiliary lubrication systems. The forward transmission oil pump is located at the bottom of the transmission, while the aft oil pump is set on the accessory gearbox. Lubrication filters are fitted with impending bypass indicators, which monitor the pressure of the oil passing through the filter to indicate if there is a blockage developing. At differential pressures of 25–30psi, the oil will be redirected to bypass the filter altogether.

The fore and aft transmissions also perform some duties other than gearing for the rotors. The aft transmission in turn drives two AC generators, the utility system pump (supplying hydraulic power to various parts of the aircraft) and the No 2 flight control hydraulic pump. The

forward transmission gives power for the No 1 flight control hydraulic pump.

One important point to note about the Chinook's rotor system is that should both engines fail, the rotors auto-rotate to enable the pilot to attempt some degree of controlled landing. The auto-rotating blades will prevent the helicopter from dropping from the sky, and the pilot can use the thrust and cyclic to flare the Chinook and make a safe, albeit bumpy, landing.

BELOW This diagram of the Textron Lycoming T55 714 shows the rotational directions of key components in the engine, including the discs in the turbine section at the rear. *(US Army)*

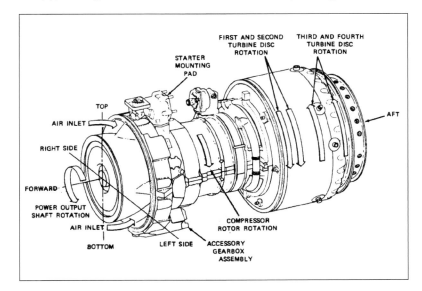

Chapter Four

Chinook in action

The Chinook has been battle-tested in the most extreme environments imaginable, and against a variety of conventional and irregular enemies. Although this experience has showed that the Chinook is far from invulnerable, it has demonstrated that the essential design embodies tactical utility and excellent survivability.

OPPOSITE A dramatic image of the Chinook releasing flares, viewed through the open rear ramp. The flares serve to confuse heat-seeking missile tracking. *(Crown Copyright)*

US combat experience – Vietnam

Although this book is primarily focused on the Chinook in RAF service, a chapter devoted to the Chinook's combat service would be incomplete without reflecting on the aircraft's use by the United States in Vietnam, for Vietnam would be the conflict in which the Chinook's tactical and logistical parameters were explored and set.

The CH-47 was present virtually from the outset of the Vietnam War. Major Chinook deployments in 1965 – the year in which the United States began making its unequivocal armed commitment – included a CH-47 battalion within 1st Cavalry Division and the 147th Aviation Medium Company, working in support of the 1st Infantry Division. These Chinooks were the tip of the iceberg: by the end of the war some 750 CH-47s had been deployed in US or South Vietnamese service. Such were the risks of the work they undertook that some 200 were lost, either through enemy fire or from operational accidents.

So what work did they perform? Most of the missions were troop or equipment deployments, especially in the resupply of remote US firebases, special forces camps and infantry outposts. The logistical operations involved a steep learning curve for all involved with the aircraft, and particularly those on the ground. Although the A, B and C models deployed to Vietnam had pretty much the same physical dimensions and cargo space as the helicopters operating today, the power plants were far less effective, especially in the hot-and-high conditions encountered in Vietnam's mountainous interior. In such locations, the total

LEFT A classic role of the CH-47 in Vietnam was helicopter recovery. Here we see a UH-1 dangling from the centre hook of a CH-47; note also the M-60 gunner on the ramp. *(DOD)*

payload was around 7,000lb (3,181kg), climbing to 10,000lb (4,545kg) over lowland areas. Infantry logistical personnel often had to be restrained by Chinook crews from overloading the temptingly capacious cabin. Nevertheless, the Chinooks were undoubted workhorses. During the Battle of the Ia Drang Valley in November 1965, US helicopter aviation shifted 13,000 tons of cargo to front-line troops, much of this performed by the CH-47s or the other great lifting helicopter of the war, the CH-54 Tarhe (or Skycrane). (Eventually the CH-54 was largely replaced by the Chinook in the theatre.) The lift capability of the Chinook also enabled it to do specialist tasks such as recover downed aircraft (some 12,000 aircraft were recovered by Chinooks during the war in what were called 'Pipe Smoke' raids) or carry artillery pieces, while entire infantry battalions could become airmobile through the Chinook.

The CH-47's ability to haul guns was one of its defining roles in Vietnam. US Army and Marine Corps firebases were often located in remote highland regions, a few hundred

ABOVE A CH-47 lands on the deck of the USS *Hancock* **during the US evacuation operations in South Vietnam in 1975, at the end of a seminal conflict for the Chinook.** *(DOD)*

LEFT A US Navy Piasecki HUP helicopter conducts a mail run to USS *Salem* **in 1957. The CH-47 was not the only operational tandem-rotor helicopter in operation during the post-war decades.** *(DOD)*

ABOVE A CH-47 Chinook at the Army Museum, Hanoi, Vietnam. During the Vietnam War, the Chinook offered a huge logistical reach, particularly to remote firebases and special forces camps. *(calflier001)*

There were experiments, however, in equipping CH-47s for far more aggressive roles in Vietnam. For example, in late 1965 Boeing-Vertol created four armed and armoured ACH-47s as assault gunships. The firepower attached to the airframe for this variant was formidable – an M5 40mm automatic grenade launcher just beneath the nose; two 2.75in rocket pods or two 7.62mm Miniguns (one each side); two fixed forward-firing 20mm cannon (one each side); four 7.62mm M60 machine guns operated from the cabin by flank gunners (two each side); and an aft gunner with either an M60 or a .50-calibre Browning machine gun.

The ACH-47 was undoubtedly a ferocious helicopter when employed in assault, but the size of its airframe and its relatively low altitude of operation made it unsuited for unilateral assault missions. Furthermore, the introduction of the Huey Cobra – a nimble and fast gunship ideally suited to rapid assault roles in support of UH-1 Huey troopships – meant that in 1967 the ACH-47 was discontinued.

Although the Vietnam War ended in 1975 (in 1973 for the US armed forces), and in defeat for the United States and South Vietnam, the Chinook had been an unequivocal success in combat service. By now the CH-47 had also passed into British service, and just a few years after the end of the Vietnam War the RAF would also get to combat test its Chinooks.

BELOW Troops make a rapid exit from the back of an HC-2 Chinook during a training exercise. Infantry often fan out to provide perimeter security for the helicopter as it lifts off. *(Crown Copyright)*

square metres of dusty land scraped from the surface of a jungle-covered mountain. It took on average about six Chinook trips to establish a battery of six 105mm howitzers, plus enough ammunition for two days of firing. (The tasking would require regular additional loads, however, for all the essentials of establishing a firebase, from the generators necessary to run electrical equipment through to the rations and mail for the men.)

The Falklands War

The war in the Falkland Islands in 1982 brought the British armed forces a logistical nightmare. The distance between the UK and the Falklands was more than 8,000 miles (12,870km), so everything that would be needed to reclaim the islands would have to be transported by the ships of a rapidly assembled task force.

A key concern of the British military planners was the most effective way to move troops and supplies rapidly around the islands once they had landed on the north-east corner of East Falkland. The solution to this problem was to be found in five HC-1 Chinooks of No 18 Squadron. To get them down to the Falklands, they were stowed aboard the 14,500-ton cargo ship *Atlantic Conveyor*, alongside six Wessex helicopters of 848 Naval Air Squadron. Having sailed from the UK on 25 April, *Atlantic Conveyor* first stopped at Ascension Island – a midpoint British supply base – where one of the Chinooks was offloaded for operations there, while the ship also took on eight Fleet Air Arm Sea Harriers and five RAF GR.3 Harriers. The heavily loaded vessel then made its way to the Falklands, arriving off the islands in mid-May, where the jets were offloaded to the carriers HMS *Hermes* and HMS *Invincible*. (No 18 Squadron engineers were far from idle on the journey – while at sea they managed to refit the rotor blades of two of the Chinooks.)

Disaster struck from across the grey South Atlantic waters on 25 May 1982. On that day, two AM39 Exocet anti-ship missiles, fired from Argentine Super Etendards at distant range, ploughed into the side of the *Atlantic Conveyor*, resulting in huge detonations and consuming fires. In the destruction of the ship, three of the four Chinooks were lost, an aching blow to the logistical capabilities of the British Falklands campaign. Note that not only were the aircraft

ABOVE An industrious group of RAF engineers perform a rotor-blade change on the deck of the *Atlantic Conveyor*, somewhere in the Atlantic in 1982. *(Crown Copyright)*

BELOW The ill-fated *Atlantic Conveyor* transport ship in 1982, seen with its load of Chinooks and Wessex helicopters on deck, most of which would be lost when the ship was sunk. *(Crown Copyright)*

Of all the helicopters in the RAF's Chinook fleet, none have the back history of Bravo November, which, in 1982, found itself a totally isolated aircraft, the sole survivor of four No 18 Squadron helicopters tragically lost many thousands of miles from home. Yet despite the complete lack of materiel support the helicopter and its crew now faced, its contribution to the British campaign in the Falklands was remarkable, and it was put to heavy use doing all the things at which a Chinook excels. Indeed, by the end of the conflict it had hauled no fewer than 1,500 British troops, 95 casualties, 650 POWs and 550 tons of cargo, in the process making a very direct contribution to the success of the British land campaign. On 2 June, for example, it transported no fewer than 85 British paratroopers from Goose Green to Fitzroy in one trip, more than doubling the recommended troop capacity. As if this were not enough, it then returned to Goose Green to transport another 75.

Yet the conflict also brought some scrapes for Bravo November. While on a night mission, Squadron Leader Dick Langworthy and his co-pilot Flight Lieutenant Andy Lawless were caught in a typically horrendous Falklands snow storm that reduced visibility to virtually nothing. The pilots decided to reduce altitude, but a faulty altimeter resulted in flying the helicopter straight into the sea at a speed of 100 knots, as Lawless later recalled:

'We were lucky, because if we had hit solid ground we would have been dead. We hit at 100 knots. The bow wave came over the cockpit window as we settled and the engines partially flamed out. I knew we had ditched, but I was not sure if we had been hit. Dick said he thought we had been hit by ground fire. As the helicopter settled, the bow wave reduced. We had the collective still up and the engine wound up as we came out of the water like a cork out of a bottle. We were climbing!' (http://www.raf.mod.uk/news/royalairforcech47chinookbravonovember.cfm.)

BELOW The famous Chinook ZA718 Bravo November, seen here in polished condition, plus the other great helicopter of the Falklands War, the Sea King, which was primarily used in a search and rescue role. *(PRMAVIA Collection)*

This remarkable incident demonstrates both the skill of the RAF pilots and the inveterate toughness of the Chinook. The impact on the sea resulted in some repairable damage to the fuselage, a ripped-off radio antenna and a lost co-pilot's door, but the helicopter was ultimately patched up and returned to operational duties. Langworthy was awarded the Distinguished Flying Cross (DFC) for his efforts in piloting the Chinook in the Falklands.

The helicopter flew throughout the conflict and well beyond. On 20 March 2003, for example, it and other Chinooks, plus RAF Pumas, took a vanguard role in the British element of the Coalition invasion of Iraq, flying from HMS *Hermes* and Kuwait to land Royal Marines on the Al-Faw peninsula. The Marines' job was to secure oil-pumping facilities on the peninsula in a night action, and the rapid insertion of the troops by the helicopters ensured that this was accomplished.

Bravo November has also served with distinction in the Afghanistan conflict. Three

of its aircrew were awarded DFCs for bravery, while the helicopter continued to provide critical resupply and transportation to front-line troops, often under great danger. All those who have flown Bravo November, however, are quick to point out that in Afghanistan all RAF Chinooks demonstrate similar mechanical endurance and all crews act with bravery.

ABOVE A crewman of ZA718 – aka Bravo November – presents something of an odd character from a fuselage window. *(Crown Copyright)*

LEFT A Chinook lands on the deck of a ship, possibly *Atlantic Conveyor*, during the Falklands campaign, 1982. Not only did the RAF lose three Chinooks in the war, but also most of their engineering kit for the helicopters. *(Crown Copyright)*

destroyed, but also all the aircraft spares and engineering equipment that went with them. One aircraft, however, the famous Bravo November, survived the destruction by virtue of being airborne at the time, being engaged in picking up cargo from HMS *Glasgow*. With its original landing platform denied, Bravo November was redirected to HMS *Hermes* whereafter it served throughout the Falklands conflict (see feature box).

The 1980s and the First Gulf War

After the Falklands, the Chinooks settled back into peacetime duties at Odiham, punctuated by exercises and training in foreign locations, such as Jordan. (Note that two Chinooks stayed on in the Falklands as part of the Falklands garrison.) Yet a politically unsettled world meant peace wouldn't last for long. In 1983, No 7 Squadron Chinooks conducted resupply missions from Akrotiri, Cyprus, to British troops conducting peacekeeping actions in Lebanon. Chinooks would also perform extensive duties in Northern Ireland during the 'Troubles', flying out to troops in remote

bases and deploying forces into contested rural regions. (Although the conflict in Northern Ireland has been largely resolved, Chinooks have still made some unexpected returns to the province. In March 2013 two Chinooks deployed from RAF Odiham to Northern Ireland in order to deliver fodder for beleaguered livestock stranded by heavy snow in Antrim and County Down.)

In 1988 an unexpected and dreadful duty for the Chinooks came on the night of 21 December 1988, after a terrorist bomb brought down Pan Am Flight 103, a Boeing 747 on a transatlantic flight from Frankfurt to Detroit. The aircraft was destroyed over Scotland, with much of the debris crashing into the small town of Lockerbie. Total death toll, including 11 people on the ground, was 270. An RAF Chinook was rapidly deployed from Odiham to Lockerbie, to help with the process of spotting and collecting the dead.

This episode, while on a truly dreadful scale, reminds us that those who crew Chinooks get closer to the horrors of war and violence than even many ground troops. It is a sombre fact that as useful as the helicopters are in transporting fit and wounded men around the battlefield, they

are also ideally suited to carrying the dead, with all the psychological stress that induces.

Within two years of the horrors of Lockerbie, the RAF Chinooks were being deployed to a more conventional conflict, this time in the Middle East. Saddam Hussein's invasion of Kuwait on 2 August 1990 precipitated a massive international response, which would boil over into an outright coalition war against Iraqi forces in 1991. Here the RAF's regular training in Jordan would pay direct dividends. By mid-January 1991, a total of 12 RAF Chinooks had been deployed as part of the vast coalition air fleet. The Pumas and Chinooks of Operation *Granby* were principally deployed forward at Jubail, and they launched into their classic logistical duties, performing resupply missions, troop deployments and casualty evacuations.

In total the Chinooks undertook some 700 sorties during Operation *Granby*, but while most flights were vital utility operations, a significant proportion involved insertions of forces deep within Iraq and occupied Kuwait.

Chinook crewman David McMullon's account of his time in the Gulf War is fascinating for providing one of the few textual accounts of Chinook responses to direct SAM threats. He

ABOVE A Chinook sits in the snow on the Falkland Islands in 1982. Note the engine intake covers and rotor tie-down straps to prevent blade movement in the windy conditions.

BELOW A Chinook HC-1 lands near a group of Iraqi Army prisoners, captured in February 1991 during Operation Desert Storm. As well as supporting logistics, the Chinooks in the Gulf War had a key role in SF insertions and extractions. *(PRMAVIA Collection)*

explains how, during one low-altitude mission, the helicopter crested a rise and the cockpit was immediately filled with the shrill beep of the RWR set, indicating that an offensive radar had the helicopter 'locked-up'. The continuous beep indicated that the enemy radar system was focused specifically on the Chinook, while the line indicator on the RWR showed that the source of the radar was coming from a four o'clock position. Fearing that the radar signature could be the prelude to a SAM attack, the pilot broke right and dropped very low – 'below sixty feet' – and performed a 'Zero Doppler Notch': by flying backwards and forwards at a right-angle to the radar beam's emission, the Chinook pilot is able to confuse the radar's ability to deduct the speed of the aircraft and whether it is flying towards or away from the radar location. (The radar is better able to measure the velocity of the helicopter if it was flying at a more acute angle to the radar beam.) At the same time, the pilot lessened the Chinook's potential missile signature by

lowering the collective, thus reducing the heat emissions from the engines.

The next counter measure deployed by the Chinook was to launch chaff and flares. Chaff – effectively a cloud of tin-foil strips – has the purpose of confusing enemy radar by creating a cloud of multiple signatures, masking the helicopter within the cloud. The flares, by contrast, created heat sources that can draw away a heat-seeking missile if fired. McMullon noted: 'We fired five flares at three-second intervals. Each one emitted such an intense heat for two or three seconds it might be enough to confuse the missile – if it was a heat signature SAM 7.' Terrain screening – hiding behind a large landscape feature to shield the helicopter – was not an option, given that the landscape around was so flat. Whatever the nature of the threat deployed against the helicopter, the defensive measures worked, and the helicopter escaped the lock-on without incident.

Although the Gulf War Chinooks were not deployed in a gunship capacity, the fact remained

ABOVE A group of Chinooks prepare to take off in sequence from a desert airfield in Iraq in 2003. A C-130 Hercules lifts off in the background, the heavier element of RAF logistics. *(PRMAVIA Collection)*

that their firepower could make a meaningful impact on the battlefield when deployed. Chinook weapon operators engaged direct threats and targets of opportunity during their flights. The M134 Minigun had a particularly devastating effect on enemy troops and vehicles, and also provided some serious backup firepower for troops being deployed or extracted by the Chinooks.

A total of 12 HC-2s from Nos 7, 18 and 27 Squadrons served in the First Gulf War, oiling the wheels of British operations in this broad theatre. A Chinook even flew in troops to secure the British Embassy in Kuwait City, once Iraqi forces had been ejected from the capital. With the conclusion of hostilities, Chinooks were then put to work ferrying essential humanitarian supplies to the Kurdish people of northern Iraq.

THE MULL OF KINTYRE CRASH

One of the most controversial and unpleasant incidents in the Chinook's history occurred on 2 June 1994, over the Mull of Kintyre in Scotland. An HC-2 Chinook, serial number ZD576, and piloted by SF pilots Flight Lieutenants Jonathan Tapper and Rick Cook, was flying from Aldergrove to Inverness carrying not only its four crew but also 25 British intelligence personnel. The helicopter ran into conditions of intense fog around the Mull of Kintyre, and tragically flew into a hillside, killing everyone on board in a devastating impact. The status of the personnel on board led to speculation about the cause of the crash, including some theories that it had been downed by a SAM missile fired by the Irish Republican Army (IRA). A subsequent RAF review, however, defined the cause as gross negligence on the part of the pilots, although this verdict in turn was questioned by subsequent military and parliamentary committees. Some authorities had blamed the crash on mechanical failure, including problems with the helicopter's FADEC system and its tactical navigation unit. The Chinooks at this time were not fitted with flight data and cockpit voice recorders, so the ultimate cause of the crash is likely to remain forever a mystery.

ABOVE An 18 Squadron Chinook in Kurdistan in 1991, seen during the vital humanitarian operations Chinooks performed there following the First Gulf War. *(PRMAVIA Collection)*

LEFT A Chinook flies over a desert air base. Maximum speed of the Chinook is around 183mph (295kph). *(Crown Copyright)*

OPPOSITE TOP This image of Chinooks and Merlins in Afghanistan in February 2007 quickly suggests the austerity Chinook crews and their engineering support experience while on deployment. *(PRMAVIA Collection)*

OPPOSITE BOTTOM The Chinook can take troops to the most inaccessible locations, in this case a Royal Marines unit to a mountainous region of Afghanistan in February 2007. *(PRMAVIA Collection)*

Peacekeeping and humanitarian ops

Even removing the Gulf War from the equation, the 1990s were a busy time for the RAF Chinooks. In the mid-1990s, the former state of Yugoslavia fractured into one of the bloodiest civil wars in recent European history. The United Nations and NATO were drawn into the Balkans in a humanitarian and eventually combative role, and with it came Odiham's Chinooks, HC-2s acting as the heavy-lift component of 24 Airmobile Brigade. Following the signing of the Dayton Peace Accords by the warring parties in 1995, RAF Chinooks alongside Royal Navy Sea Kings were

used to deploy artillery pieces into north-west Bosnia, as part of the process of establishing an Implementation Force (IFOR) buffer zone between the warring parties in that part of the country. The Chinooks were also involved in the process of assisting engineering efforts to rebuild the shattered country, and conducted humanitarian supply missions into Banja Luka, Bosnia, to Serbian refugees.

In 1997 the situation in the Balkans suddenly deteriorated with the collapse of Albania. A new air of emergency was added by the fact that British civilians living in Albania suddenly came under threat, and needed rapid evacuation. In several cases the Chinook was the delivery vehicle for troops performing the extractions. In late March 1997, for example, two Chinooks were sent into Albania with a force from the Prince of Wales Royal Regiment, to establish a safe extraction site for troops that had driven into Albania to rescue a British aid worker, Robert Welch. The next day, Chinooks acted as an escort force for a column of rescuers, two British aid workers and the 22 Romanian children under their care.

The Balkans kept the RAF's Chinooks busy right until the end of the 1990s, not least as Kosovo became a fresh war zone. At the beginning of June 1999, No 7 Squadron Chinooks deployed troops into Kosovo to observe the situation there, and eight Chinooks of the Support Helicopter Force (SHF) were moved into southern Macedonia, based at Prilep, as replacements for those that had been operating over Bosnia. These helicopters would provide a support element for the invasion of Kosovo by the 5th Airborne Brigade, as Yugoslavian forces began their evacuation. The SHF then moved up to Camp Piper, north of Skopje.

The main objective of the British component of the invasion was to secure and defend the Kacanik defile, and the Chinooks were to be in the lead of the operation. It began at 0500 hours on 12 June 1999, with eight troop- and vehicle-carrying Chinooks crossing the border into Kosovo as part of the major coalition effort. With all the key points secured on the 12th, the next day Chinooks deployed British paratroopers into Pristina, as Yugoslavian forces finally left the capital.

BELOW An RAF Chinook prepares to lift a Ferret armoured car in 1982, during peacekeeping and evacuation operations in the Lebanon. Note the searchlight fitting beneath the nose.
(Crown Copyright)

LEFT During operations in Kosovo in the 1990s, a Chinook lifts a section of pontoon bridge; note how the length of the cargo requires all three hook points. *(Crown Copyright)*

LEFT In an astonishing demonstration of flying precision, Chinooks deploy British troops to a bridge over the Kacanik Pass, Kosovo, during operations in 1999. *(Crown Copyright)*

ABOVE HC-2 Chinooks lift off after deploying British soldiers into a field in Kosovo, during operations in the country in the late 1990s. The helicopter's weapons support officer (WSO), with M134 Minigun, is visible in the starboard door. *(Crown Copyright)*

RIGHT Taken in Kosovo, this dramatic photograph shows the Chinook carrying an extended vehicle. The knotted rope allows the crewmen better control of the cable. *(Crown Copyright)*

Operations in Africa

Britain's Chinook force has to be ready to deploy around the world at a moment's notice, as events in 2000 in Sierra Leone demonstrated. Sierra Leone had been blighted by civil war since 1991, but in early May 2000 the British military was forced to intervene as the rebel Revolutionary United Front (RUF) – a group known for its atrocities – began to advance on the capital, Freetown. British and other foreign nationals were at risk, so by 7 May 1st Battalion, the Parachute Regiment, had deployed to secure evacuation areas in Freetown and also Lunghi airport, the main route of egress from the country for the foreign nationals.

Chinooks would be critical to the evacuation operation, as the principal means of transferring the evacuees from Freetown to Lunghi Airport.

Four HC-2s from all three Chinook squadrons were chosen for the mission. The problem

was getting them there. At that point in time, there were no external means available for the Chinooks to be transferred to Sierra Leone. Yet the clock was ticking, so the conclusion was inevitable – the Chinooks would have to get themselves to Africa. Thus the four aircraft, in staged journeys, flew the 3,000 miles (4,827km) to Sierra Leone, a journey that took them three days. The trip would be the longest undertaken by Chinooks in their operational history.

RIGHT A shipborne Chinook. The wedge-shaped feature under the centre of the nose is the housing for the aircraft's radar warning receiver (RWR). *(Crown Copyright)*

ABOVE Seen during the 1980s, a Chinook sits on an airfield while a Harrier V/STOL (vertical/short take-off and landing aircraft) touches down nearby. *(Crown Copyright)*

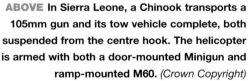

ABOVE In Sierra Leone, a Chinook transports a 105mm gun and its tow vehicle complete, both suspended from the centre hook. The helicopter is armed with both a door-mounted Minigun and ramp-mounted M60. *(Crown Copyright)*

ABOVE The gun and truck combination is deposited on a road in front of an amazed crowd. The lifting power of the Chinook means that ready-to-fight loads such as this can be transported in an assembled state. *(Crown Copyright)*

Once the Chinooks were in Sierra Leone they began their work as part of Operation *Palliser*, helping to evacuate some 500 people over the course of a week. Yet this was only the beginning of No 7 Squadron's involvement in Sierra Leone. The helicopters were engaged in many troop-ferrying actions, both of British soldiers and of United Nations Mission in Sierra Leone (UNAMSIL) reinforcements being flown into the country, as the RUF once more began to gather its strength. On 7 July two Chinooks worked with Indian troops to extract Major Andy Harrison, a United Nations Military Observer (UNMO), plus several other UNMOs and a

handful of combat-wounded Gurkhas, from an RUF-besieged base at Kailahun.

A more sizeable and dangerous operation was Operation *Barras*. Eleven soldiers of the Royal Irish Regiment (RIR), attached to UNAMSIL, had been taken prisoner on 25 August by a vicious militia group known as the West Side Boys. They were held in the village of Gberi Bana, and over the next few days the British negotiators managed to secure the release of all but five of the men. Yet the mental state of the West Side Boys, and their leader, Foday Kallay, began to deteriorate along with the negotiations, and so the British

LEFT This RAF Chinook, date and location unknown, is possibly part of an SF flight, given its extensive camouflage covering. Machine-gun casing vents are seen under the starboard door, but no weapon appears to be fitted. *(Crown Copyright)*

LEFT The nose of an HC-2 Chinook, with HMS *Fearless* in the background. This view shows, to good effect, the helicopter's RWR housing and the twin pitot tube housings with vertical aerials. *(Crown Copyright)*

RIGHT Troops prepare to board a Chinook near Sierra Leone. Note how the engine exhausts vent safely (albeit noisily) over the heads of the soldiers. *(Crown Copyright)*

decided that the RIR soldiers needed rescuing – Operation *Barras*.

The Chinooks worked hard over the combat areas throughout the mission, transferring out the British soldiers as they completed their missions and also taking on board the dead and wounded. (One British soldier was killed and twelve wounded during the action.) The helicopters even managed to airlift out the RIR's captured Land Rover

vehicles, taking them out as underslung loads.

The British operations in Sierra Leone were further vindication – if it were needed – of the tactical value of the Chinook helicopter. Yet even though the 1990s and first year of the 2000s had been a busy one for the RAF Chinooks, few could have foretold the escalation of operational requirements that would soon be placed upon the Odiham crews.

RIGHT A fine view of a Chinook making a ship deck-landing, the No 2 crewman at the starboard door calling fine adjustments to the pilot. *(Crown Copyright)*

RIGHT Despite their size, Chinooks have the precision-flying capabilities to perform shipboard operations. Here a Chinook lifts off from the deck of a carrier, behind a Sea King search and rescue helicopter. *(Crown Copyright)*

Afghanistan

The world's security picture changed dramatically on 11 September 2001 with the terrorist attacks on the World Trade Center in New York and the Pentagon. Afghanistan became the primary focus for the international response, and British forces were being deployed into the country alongside US and other coalition troops by the end of the year.

For effective military operations, Afghanistan was a country that virtually demanded the

BELOW A Chinook performs a tactical demonstration. A strop has just been attached to a Land Rover; many infantrymen are trained to be 'hookers' to attach loads to hovering Chinooks. *(Crown Copyright)*

use of the Chinook. The road network was generally primitive, the distances great, and the terrain variable (from desert-like plains to towering mountains, depending on the part of the country in which troops were operating). The Chinook enabled the British troops to move rapidly around the country, and made remote forward operating bases (FOBs) viable

through the helicopters' resupply capabilities. Troops could be given deep-penetration mobility throughout the country by the Chinook. Most important, the Chinook provided the means to take medical emergency response teams (MERTs) to the battlefield to extract wounded soldiers.

The RAF Chinooks worked in support of various operations from late 2001 to June 2002, collaborating with US and coalition forces in various aggressive sweep actions in remote contested regions of Afghanistan, especially around the Afghan–Pakistan border. Since June 2002, however, the British part of International Security Assistance Force (ISAF) operations in Afghanistan has been designated Operation *Herrick*, primarily focused on providing security, rebuilding and combat missions in Helmand Province, southern Afghanistan, with other British troops also in Kandahar and Kabul.

Herrick has drawn heavily upon Odiham's 18 (B) and 27 Squadron Chinooks, these being operated by RAF 1310 Flight as the heavy-lift element of the Joint Helicopter Force (Afghanistan) – JHF(A) – based in Kandahar and Camp Bastion. Along with the Hercules transporters of the RAF 904 Expeditionary Air Wing (EAW), 1310 Flight has provided airlift capability to thousands of troops and equally thousands of tonnes of cargo. Flight

BELOW Troops wait for embarkation instructions from a crewman during Exercise Jebel Sahara, an annual exercise, in North Africa. *(Crown Copyright)*

deployments to Afghanistan, based on Kandahar or Camp Bastion, typically lasted 13 weeks, with 12 weeks of operations and a thirteenth week devoted to handover procedures to the replacement flight. The following 38 weeks were then spent either away on training and exercise, on standby ops and routine flying at Odiham, on annual leave, on career courses or even (for a lucky few), adventure training. In this way, the start of each spell in Afghanistan rolled back a couple of months each year, ensuring a change of season and probably a change in the intensity of action.

It would take an entire book of its own to do justice to more than a decade of Chinook operations in Afghanistan. Suffice to say that Afghanistan has stretched the Chinook and its crews to the very limits of operational endurance and performance. Furthermore, the survivability of the Chinook has been extraordinary, given the fact that it flies into harm's way on an almost daily basis. A single Chinook has been shot down – it was hit by

enemy fire in August 2009, caught fire, and crashed north of Sangin. The damage resulted in the helicopter having to make a high-impact landing, which effectively destroyed the aircraft, although all on board survived and were immediately recovered by another helicopter. The shattered Chinook on the ground, however, was subsequently destroyed by a coalition airstrike to prevent anything valuable falling into enemy hands. Continuing a bad month, later in August another Chinook was forced to make a hard landing and was also later destroyed.

ABOVE A Chinook fires flares as it comes in to land in Helmand, Afghanistan. Landing is a vulnerable phase for the aircraft, as it reduces the distance between the helicopter and ground threats. *(Crown Copyright)*

RIGHT Troops aboard a Chinook in Afghanistan. Note how all their weapons point downwards, away from vital aircraft components, in case there is an accidental discharge. *(Crown Copyright)*

At least four months before these incidents, it was revealed that the Taliban were specifically planning to down a Chinook, principally by using twin 14.5mm cannon mounted on the backs of trucks. Most of these weapon systems were subsequently destroyed by airstrikes, but the losses in August showed that, despite their resilience, the Chinooks were still vulnerable.

Here we shall look at some examples of specific missions, as well as examine some notable incidents in which Chinooks have excelled, either in mechanical resilience or in human bravery.

RPG impact

One of the most astonishing episodes for the Chinook in the Afghan war occurred to Flight Lieutenant Alex 'Frenchie' Duncan, a Chinook pilot in No 27 Squadron, in May 2008 during operations over Helmand. It was an incident that subsequently received huge press coverage, with the benefit of highlighting the extraordinary capabilities of both the Chinook and the crews who operate it.

The mission was a straightforward one – a three-Chinook flight from Camp Bastion to Lashkar Gah, where they would pick up some cargo and personnel, then perform some further runs to Musa Qala before return to base. Throughout the first phases of the day, Duncan noted that ICOM (intelligence communication) chatter – essentially radio transmissions intercepted from the Taliban – increased in intensity, a worrying sign that the enemy was up to something.

To increase security, Duncan took the helicopter into Musa Qala via a different route

than he took previously, as the Taliban would post insurgents on the expected flight paths with the hope of successfully engaging a Chinook. He made the approach to Musa Qala through a deep wadi that ran past nearby FOB Edinburgh, flying at just feet from the ground with the terrain providing shelter. During the approach, however, Duncan suddenly spotted a Toyota Hilux vehicle by the side of the wadi, with a man standing in the back. Fearing that the truck was the platform for an attack, Duncan immediately threw the helicopter out to the left. As it turned out, the truck was actually no threat at all, but the evasive manoeuvre took the helicopter low over a Taliban ambush team, which opened up with small-arms fire and RPGs. The Chinook was hit by both, and an RPG round actually passed through the aircraft rear pylon without detonating, before hitting and exploding on the rotor blades. Duncan, in his excellent book *Sweating the Metal*, vividly describes his struggle to control the Chinook:

'The Master Caution goes off and I'm thrust into a world of *son et lumière*. Warning lights are flashing and the rad alt alarm is sounding through my helmet speakers.

'"Mayday! Mayday! Mayday! Black Cat Two Two, Mayday. We've been hit!" says Alex over the radio. Then "Frenchie, we've lost the No 2 hydraulic system and the AFCS, both secured."

'"It could be worse," I think. The AFCS is an auto-stabiliser that helps to keep the aircraft straight and level, but I can fly without it. The No 2 hydraulic system is more of a concern, but it's not life-and-death. The real concern is the blade; I've no idea how badly damaged it is, or how long it will last.

'I push the cyclic forward and amazingly the cab responds. Something is seriously wrong though; it's woolly and there's a lag to my input. The aircraft is shaking like a bastard; the pedals are shaking, the cyclic is vibrating in my hand. The aircraft feels completely wrong as I'm trying to fly her; the rear is skidding – a sign of a big imbalance there. It's the rotor head telling me it's missing a piece.' (*Sweating the Metal*, p.223.)

Duncan considered putting the seriously damaged aircraft down immediately, but that would put his crew and the 16 civilian passengers on board into hostile territory, with only a handful of rifles on board to provide defence. As if to

reinforce that this wasn't an option, another RPG missile shot past the helicopter. So instead, Duncan headed for nearby FOB Edinburgh, gaining emergency clearance for landing. Through dextrous flying, and the resilience of the Chinook, Duncan managed to make his landing in a cloud of grit and dust, much to the relief of crew and passengers.

Once on the ground, Duncan had the opportunity to inspect the damage, which was sobering to see. There was a total of 34 holes in the aircraft, from shrapnel and 7.62mm and .50-cal rounds. (A .50-cal round had even hit the gearbox, but it had bounced off!) Most shocking, however, was the RPG strike. This had entered the aft pylon and exited to strike one of the rotor blades, tearing a huge chunk out of it. Incredibly, the whole system kept its integrity, and got the Chinook to FOB Edinburgh. For his skill and bravery that day, Duncan was awarded the Distinguished Flying Cross.

What makes this incident more remarkable is that it was not isolated. More than two years later, on the morning of 15 December 2010, Duncan awoke at Camp Bastion and set out to investigate the day's operational demands. The expectation was that he would be flying 'taskings', routine missions deploying cargo or troops, rather than be on the potential

ABOVE A MERT treats a casualty aboard a Chinook in Afghanistan. The MERT team focuses on immediate stabilisation of the casualty and, if need be, preparing him/her for emergency surgery. *(Crown Copyright)*

ABOVE UK troops leave Forward Operating Base (FOB) Shawqat, Helmand Province, for the last time by Chinook helicopter in August 2013. *(Crown Copyright)*

RIGHT A Chinook helicopter above the Nahr-e Saraj South district of Helmand Province, the photo clearly demonstrating the issues of rotor erosion from dust particles. *(Crown Copyright)*

adrenaline trips of IRT (incident response team). His co-pilot was Flight Lieutenant Andrew 'Waldo' Waldron. At the JOC (joint operations centre) tent he received his missions – he and a wingman were to transport underslung loads (USLs) to FOB Kalaang, perform troop/cargo movements between several patrol bases (PBs) and Bastion, and fly some RAF personnel from Bastion to Kandahar Airfield (KAF). A busy day, but also one made notable by two distinct operational changes:

'Whereas on all previous Dets, we've flown all but the most vital of our sorties at night, we're flying by day this time. Secondly, and perhaps most controversially, the threat assessment for all HLSs [helicopter landing sites] has been downgraded by the powers that be due to "lack of enemy activity". To my mind, this lack of activity reflects the quality of the tactics that we in the Chinook Force employ. The fact that we have previously flown to the most dangerous landing sites in the wee small hours of the morning to accomplish our taskings was largely down to the simple fact that there was less enemy activity then because Terry Taliban was asleep.' (Ibid, p.298.)

The run to Kalaang was a smooth trip. The Chinook, as on so many missions in Afghanistan, was accompanied by an Apache gunship. Having Apaches working in tandem with the Chinooks meant that the larger transport helicopters had recourse to some serious firepower, should they run into trouble. During the first trip back to Bastion, Duncan did overhear radio chatter between the Apache and the joint terminal attack controller (JTAC), discussing the fact that a Chinook had been engaged with small-arms fire.

With this ominous sign in mind, Duncan's Chinook and another flown by Flight Lieutenant Pete Amstutz and Flight Lieutenant Doug 'Snoop Dog' Gardner returned to Bastion, collected further loads, and headed out to Patrol Base 3 (PB3). It was over that location that the helicopters were greeted by heavy small-arms fire (known as 'SAFIRE' in radio speak), from multiple points around the patrol base. Duncan's wingman managed to complete his landing and egress, the SAFIRE subsiding significantly when an Apache provided air cover. Duncan, however, was not so lucky. Some 3km from

PB3, enemy forces engaged with SAFIRE and launched an RPG at the low-flying Chinook, the bullets striking the helicopter and the shaped-charge missile exploding beside the port door with a huge detonation. Duncan's immediate response was to 'throw the cyclic hard left and hit the USL release button; immediately, the load pings away and becomes a dumb bomb, falling to earth and who gives a f*** where it lands. My only priority is the cab and crew; I need lightness and manoeuvrability.' (Ibid, p.304.)

The battle damage produced chaos in the instrumentation, throwing out worrying problems with the No 1 engine, the fuel system, all the gearboxes and many other things. The conclusion was that the nearby RPG strike had damaged the instrumentation, but there were also increased levels of vibration in the airframe. Yet as with the incident previously described, Duncan and his crew were able to take the aircraft safely to Camp Bastion.

IRT roles

The most critical role of the Chinooks in Afghanistan has, of course, been casualty evacuation. Two Chinooks have been kept at Camp Bastion on permanent standby as incident response team (IRT) and Helmand Reaction Force (HRF) aircraft. The IRT helicopter provides an incident response team that consists of the

ABOVE A Mk 3 Chinook in flight in 2013, with a crewman performing the traditional role of voice marshalling – providing the pilots with an auditory guide to manoeuvring. *(Crown Copyright)*

land forces in Afghanistan, and also by civilians caught up in the war. Not only is it in demand (an average of four call-outs a day was not uncommon during the period 2007–11), but it frequently makes the difference between a soldier dying or living. Here a Chinook pilot explains the connection between them and the ground forces:

'I think that there is a close relationship between us and the Army, Marines and other foot soldiers because we do what we call the IRT, but what a lot of people call the medical emergency response team. It's a case that if you need us, we will be in the air within five or ten minutes, and we will come and get you, whatever the weather, even if the weather means we can barely see our hands in front of our faces. We'll do our best to get there. That capability is hugely valued by the guys on the ground out there, and I think that the fact that we have on so many occasions got guys out, who possibly without the Chinook wouldn't be here today, means that the Army are very fond of the Chinook, so much so that if you pick up a *Soldier* magazine or any other gloss military mag, it will have loads of Chinooks in it. And it is often mistaken for an Army helicopter, but they are really exclusively Royal Air Force.

'In Afghanistan, there is always one helicopter permanently set up as an IRT helicopter. The back of it is set up as a field hospital, and it is pretty much as advanced as a casualty operating room in the UK.'

ABOVE A MERT extracts a member of the Afghan Uniformed Police (AUP) after he was wounded by the detonation of an improvised explosive device (IEP), following a joint Anglo-Afghan helicopter assault mission. *(Crown Copyright)*

aircrew plus a medical emergency response team (MERT), and an RAF Regiment force protection team to provide evacuation defence. All these personnel live in close proximity to one another at Bastion, and if the emergency call comes in they can be aloft in minutes. Furthermore, the weapons support operators (WSOps – formerly known as Loadmasters, more generally known as Crewmen) in the back of the Chinook will provide physical support to the medical team when required.

The IRT Chinook is hugely valued by the

RIGHT An ambulance waits to take a casualty on board at Camp Bastion, Afghanistan. The helicopter crew will aim to get the casualty to hospital within an hour of the wounding. *(Crown Copyright)*

Another pilot with similar operational experience, interviewed by the author, added:

'Conditions for the MERT on board the Chinook are utterly demanding. The cabin can be full of dust, debris and blood, and the light levels low. The aircraft might have to perform evasive manoeuvres, throwing the cabin occupants around. I've been on aircraft where they've actually opened up guys' chests and physically started massaging guys' hearts, with dust and grit flying around – and at night, with just a little bit of light so that they can see what they're doing but not enough so that the enemy can see [the aircraft] – being thrown around all over the place because you're being shot at. To perform open-heart surgery while that's going on is just incredible.

'If you speak to any Chinook operator I think that they'll say that's the most rewarding and probably the most important job that we could ever do. And in some ways it's a job that we enjoy, because of the job satisfaction that we get out of it – the fact that we're genuinely making a difference – but at the same time it's quite a difficult job to do because we lose people, or they've suffered life-changing injuries.'

The IRT role brings with it considerable risks, as the helicopters have to fly directly into harm's way to pick up the casualties. So do the aircrew ever judge a mission too hazardous to fly? 'You have a veto on the operation, but I can't recall anybody ever using the veto as such. So normally the decision is made by the chain of command, as to which asset they're going to send depending on the nature of the injuries. And they despatch the asset – such as the Chinook. But at the point of going into that landing site there's an element of "Do I, don't I?" You won't obviously go into a scenario where you're definitely going to get shot down, because what's the point of losing the lives of 12 to save the life of one? But very rarely do you face a situation that's that clear cut.

RIGHT In Afghanistan, Chinooks from the Odiham squadrons have been kept flying on a 24/7 basis, their roles ranging from resupply to medical emergencies. *(Crown Copyright)*

BELOW Troops deploy from a Chinook in dusty conditions. The downwash of the Chinook can reduce ground visibility to nearly zero, the troops having to remain motionless until visibility returns. *(Crown Copyright)*

Normally it's more a case of going in and doing the evacuation in the safest and fastest possible way, and in the most covert way we can.'

Another pilot added, however, that the IRT Chinooks are typically not left defenceless:

'We always take an Apache with us when we do that, so when there's a known enemy position we can delay going in by five minutes or so to allow the Apache to go in and engage that specific target if it's a known, specifically identified target which they can take out. You can almost think of the Apache as our self-defence; they can just sit over the top and watch us in and we just pitch up and do everything else. It's very common to delay slightly before going in just to reduce the risk, but it's also very, very rare for someone to turn around and not go in, mainly because everyone knows that if it was us on the ground we'd want them to come and get us. The quicker you can get to someone the more likely they are to live or to keep a leg.'

Only by putting themselves in harm's way can the crews of the Chinooks perform their IRT roles. For this reason, they have the respect and affection of virtually all ground troops.

Aggressive roles

Chinooks are, as we have already seen in this chapter, often used in more combat-oriented missions. These include SF deployments and support of major airborne assaults. Chinooks have provided UK and Coalition ground forces with the ability to make surprise attacks into the most remote locations, each helicopter packed with combat-ready troops and (sometimes) vehicles.

A good example of one of these missions

RIGHT Well-disciplined British troops arrange themselves into two columns for rapid boarding of a Chinook, which is turning to present its rear door. *(Crown Copyright)*

in action is Operation *Augustus*. Launched on 14 July 2006, *Augustus* was a major combined action to capture or kill a Taliban commander north of Sangin, and defeat his personal bodyguard force, estimated to be about 50 strong. The Taliban force was believed to be holed up in a compound complex, and to tackle this objective A and C Companies, 3 Para, plus a contingent of Canadian troops, would be taken rapidly into the fight by five Chinooks, crewed by personnel from both 18 and 27 Squadron. Each of the Chinooks would be carrying around 40 fully equipped paratroopers plus a quad bike. Heavy enemy resistance was expected at the helicopter landing site (HLS), so the mission would be heavily supported by Apache gunships, a US B-1 bomber and an AC-130 gunship, to provide fire support.

Augustus was launched in the early hours on the morning of the 14th. The nine helicopters involved in the insertion initially flew away from their target for 20 minutes, a tactical measure to confuse any potential Taliban observers, and also an opportunity to test weapons over a deserted area. The helicopters then about-turned, and headed in to the HLS. Unfortunately, it became apparent over the HLS that the Taliban knew the British forces were coming, evidenced by the huge amount of fire that met the first Chinooks into the HLS. The first Chinook managed to deposit its troops without being hit, remarkably, although two RPGs bracketed the helicopter during its rapid ascent from the ground. The second Chinook, however, was hit multiple times by small-arms fire, and one of its Para occupants was wounded with a bullet to the shoulder. The third Chinook also made a successful deployment of its troops, although the mission JTAC and his signaller had to jump 15ft (4.5m) from the ramp when the helicopter began to lift off while they were still aboard.

The final two Chinooks were told to abort by the Apaches when flying into the HLS, because

of the resistance. They subsequently returned and deposited their loads, but only after the AC-130 had inflicted lethal destruction on the Taliban forces around the compound. The mission was ultimately an incredible success, with a few wounded British troops against many Taliban dead. Without the flexibility and speed of the Chinooks, such actions would scarcely be possible.

BELOW For long-range deployments, Chinooks are transported by either ship or aircraft. With its rotors removed, this HC-2 fits aboard a C-17 transporter. *(PRMAVIA Collection)*

ABOVE During Exercise Joint Winter in March 2004, a Chinook carries two 105mm light guns, the arrangement of the guns staggered to avoid their clashing in flight. *(PRMAVIA Collection)*

RIGHT An RAF Chinook in the Gulf in March 2003 transfers a netted load of cargo, passing by a flight of RAF Sea Kings warming up. *(PRMAVIA Collection)*

BELOW A Merlin and a Chinook turn rotors while on exercise in Morocco in October 2008; the Merlin is a multi-role helicopter that can carry up to 24 troops. *(PRMAVIA Collection)*

Iraq

Of course, Afghanistan was not the only war zone for the RAF Chinooks following the terrorist attacks on the United States in 2001. In 2003, Coalition forces invaded Iraq in one of the biggest military operations since the end of World War Two. Operation *Telic* – as the British contribution to the Iraq War was labelled – ran until 2011, and it relied heavily on the use of

more than 100 rotary-winged aircraft, including the Chinooks.

Helicopters were the central component of one of the opening actions of the war – the airborne assault on the al-Faw peninsula. HC-2s of 18 Squadron, flying from HMS *Ark Royal*, deployed Royal Marines directly into the oil facilities of the peninsula, and kept them resupplied as they consolidated their gains. The Chinooks would also be central to the British campaign to consolidate Basra, and even took part in the actions around Baghdad – principally a US objective.

As history now knows, although Iraq fell to the Coalition in a matter of months, the insurgency in Iraq has rumbled on in harrowing fashion to the present day. This ongoing conflict kept the Chinooks busy with the usual variety of missions. An RAF Odiham news item, written shortly before the withdrawal of British forces from Iraq, noted of 27 Squadron: 'More recently the Squadron has been deployed on Operations in Iraq supplying crews to 1310 Flight, the Chinook component of Joint Helicopter Force (Iraq). Squadron personnel regularly deploy to Basrah Air Station in Support of Multi National Division (South East). Daily tasks include troop, freight and passenger moves around theatre,

RIGHT A view looking forward through the cockpit of an HC-2; a magnetic direct-reading compass sits in the top of the dashboard. *(PRMAVIA Collection)*

Vehicle Check Point operations, supporting ground operations, under-slung load operations and "top cover"/show of force sorties. The Flight also operates at Camp Abu Naji-a Forward Operating Base at Al Amarah where crews provide a 24 hour a day, 30 minutes notice to move, Immediate Response Team. The Squadron flies over 50 sorties a month in support of Operation TELIC – the UK's continued support to rebuilding Iraq after UK/US led forces removed Saddam Hussein from power and ended his long dictatorship in Iraq.' (http://www.raf.mod.uk/RAFodiham/aboutus/27sqn.cfm.)

One particular point of interest here is the reference to vehicle checkpoint (VCP) operations. VCP actions were part of a general effort to control the movement of insurgents within contested areas. Generally, the Chinooks would airlift a section of troops to a specific VCP location, deploying the troops, who would then set up and man the checkpoint for a period of time. To ensure that the VCP was effective, and not simply avoided when emplaced, and also to increase troop security, the Chinooks would later return and move the troops to another location. This process was repeated multiple times within a single day.

Taken together, the wars in Iraq and Afghanistan have been a fundamental validation of the Chinook's role. Without the Chinook, a huge range of tactical and logistical options would simply not have been available to British forces, and hundreds of men might not be alive today. The next major combat deployment for the Chinooks is uncertain, but even in days of shrinking defence budgets, it appears that the Chinook will always be in high demand.

ABOVE A Chinook sits on the deck of aircraft carrier HMS *Invincible* in March 2004. The rotors and cockpit are both protected with anti-icing covers, as ice build-up can either prevent take-off or cause excessive engine strain in flight. *(PRMAVIA Collection)*

RIGHT This Chinook has been fitted with snow skis. Landing directly into snow without such skis can result in damage to the undercarriage from unseen objects. *(PRMAVIA Collection)*

Chapter Five

The pilot's view

Chinook pilots are a breed apart, operating a unique aircraft in testing circumstances. Unlike many other forms of military flying, Chinook pilots have to fly into the heart of the front line, enduring dangers not encountered by those at higher altitudes.

OPPOSITE The Chinook is emphatically a four-person helicopter. The pilots are only able to perform their roles with the guidance and support of the WSOs, and the WSOs are in turn dependent on the flying skill of the pilots. *(Crown Copyright)*

ABOVE A Chinook HC-2/2A of 18 (B) Squadron, flying from HMS *Ark Royal*, lifts a Lynx helicopter back to HMS *Ocean* near Cyprus during an amphibious warfare exercise, 2003. *(Crown Copyright)*

In times past, it was fast jets that caught the imagination of both the public and of those who aspired to join the RAF as pilots. Helicopter flying was somehow seen as less exciting, with its emphasis on utility and logistics, than making supersonic strike attacks in an ultra-destructive combat jet. Yet time has resulted in a distinct shift in perceptions. The war in Afghanistan in particular has placed the Chinook firmly at the centre of people's awareness about combat aviation. While the fast jets frequently sit at tens of thousands of feet altitude, delivering precision-guided munitions (PGMs), the Chinooks are seen flying straight into firefights to rescue injured crews, or making low-level insertions of assault troops. And as the public awareness of the Chinook has grown, so has the desire among many would-be pilots to join rotary-wing aviation as their first choice.

The journey to the Chinook

In an interview with the author, Flight Lieutenant Kyle Thomas, a Chinook pilot and member of the RAF's Chinook Display Team, explained how an aspiring pilot might make his way on to the Chinook:

'When you join the Royal Air Force and you sign on the dotted line, you attend officer training for a year. At the end of that, providing obviously you've been selected as a pilot, you go off to do your elementary flying training, which is on the Tutor, a single-engined piston aircraft. Now that takes six to eight months, depending on the weather, the time of year, and other factors. And once you've completed that you're streamed on your ability and on your preference to either fast jet, rotary or multi-engine transport. You give your preference of what you'd like to do, numbered from one to three. Most guys want to go for fast jets first, rotary second and multi-engine [C-130, Voyager, C-17, A400M etc] third. Some guys have no interest in helicopters, or in multis, so the authorities generally won't send you to anywhere you don't want to go if they can avoid it. So if someone finished top of their course, and doesn't want to go fast jets for some reason, and he wants to go multis, he'll generally be sent to multis. You also get crossovers of qualified pilots. Some will go from the fast-jet world to rotary, or people go from rotary to fast jet, so you get this knowledge base spread around.

'If you go down the rotary route you go to RAF Shawbury [home of the Defence Helicopter Flying School for all three military services, and the Central Flying School (Helicopter)] and you do a course that can generally take up to two years. You fly two different helicopters there. First is the Squirrel, which is the Eurocopter AS350B. You do a basic and an advanced phase on that, which obviously includes learning to fly the helicopter. The big shock initially is that compared to a fixed-wing aircraft, everything is different in a helicopter. You learn low-level flying, which on a helicopter is 50 to 100ft rather than 250ft. You do your helicopter formation flying and instrument flying.

'Then you go on to the Griffin HT1, which

The Chinook HC-2 flight simulator at RAF Benson, on which trainee pilots spend dozens of hours dealing with all manner of creative emergencies. *(Crown Copyright)*

is the Bell 412EP, at 60 Squadron (R), and that's where you learn multi-engine, multi-crew helicopter flying. You get to know the crew and also work as two pilots up front, rather than the single person you've been used to so far. A year of the two years at Shawbury is pretty much spent with 60 Squadron, first converting to a twin-engine helicopter and multi-crew, and then you go through an advanced phase of flying, which focuses more on tactical flying. Next you have an operations phase when you go off and deploy and do things like four- or five-ship airfield assaults, tasking and all the sorts of things we do on the front line.

'Then after that you get role disposed, again partially on preference but mostly on available slots and ability. The helicopters used to be Chinook, Puma, Merlin and Sea King, but the Merlin is transferring to the Royal Navy and the Sea King is being retired from service, so for the RAF it will either be the Chinook or the Puma. If you're lucky enough to end up at RAF Odiham, you come on to the Operational Conversion Flight – this should take 30 weeks. It adds

ABOVE A Chinook approaches Bagram airbase, Afghanistan. Although the HC-4 features digitised mapwork, paper maps are still routinely used on operations. *(PRMAVIA Collection)*

LEFT A Chinook and Puma in flight together. The Puma entered service in 1971 as a troop-carrying and utility helicopter, and is operated by Nos 33 and 230 Squadrons at RAF Benson. *(Crown Copyright)*

even with the changing tides in Afghanistan, that situation is unlikely to alter.

Flying the Chinook

So what is the Chinook like to fly, for those skilled and fortunate enough to make it through the long training period? Kyle Thomas explains:

'The Chinook's standard characteristics are better for the pilot than a normal helicopter, which basically is all down to the tandem-rotor design. In a normal helicopter, when you apply power or make an adjustment you get a torque reaction, so you get the tail trying to move, so there's a lot of hands and feet going on all the time to compensate. But with the Chinook, because of the tandem-rotor system, the torque effect is negated. So, for example, if you want to do a hover in a Chinook you can do it with your feet off the pedals and it will just stay pointing in the same direction – that in itself is a great ability to have. And then the AFCS system takes out all the undesirable effects of the tandem-rotor system, because it works very differently to a single-rotor helicopter. For example, if you want to go forwards in a normal helicopter, you push the cyclic forward, the disc goes forward, and you start to move forward. In a Chinook, the discs only really tilt left and right; if you want to

ABOVE Chinook pilots need ground support like any other military aviator. Here an RAF Mobile Air Operations Team leader (MAOT) observes as a Chinook helicopter takes off during Exercise *Jebel Sahara* in North Africa, 2009. *(Crown Copyright)*

up to about 150 hours in the helicopter and about 79 hours in the simulator, and hundreds of hours of ground training. The whole flying training process can take anywhere from three to five years, depending on how quickly you get through the components. The initial officer training element can take a year on top of that.'

This demanding flying programme is a huge investment on the part of the RAF. Yet as we have seen repeatedly in this book, it is a sound investment. Chinook pilots are, at the time of writing, in constant operational demand, and

RIGHT The co-pilot of a Chinook provides navigation guidance to the pilot during a training flight over Wales. The demanding terrain of Wales is ideal for instructing in a variety of tactical manoeuvres. *(Crown Copyright)*

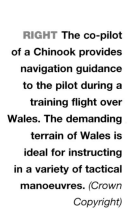

go forward it's all about the pitch on the blades. To go forward, more pitch goes on the rear head, pitch comes off the front head, and that tilts the whole helicopter forward. And then if you want to go left in a turn, both discs go sideways. If you want yaw, both discs go in separate directions and you turn around yourself.

'Another thing. When you're in a normal helicopter and you put cyclic input to turn – say if you want to put a 30° angle of bank turn on to go left or right – you have to hold that angle of bank on with the stick. So you move the stick and hold it in the position at which you want to turn. In a fixed-wing aircraft you roll on your bank and then you return the stick to the centre and the bank stays stable. The Chinook also does that. So you roll it to whatever angle of bank you want, the stick goes back to the middle like a plane, and the aircraft flies around in angle-of-bank hold. It was designed to feel more like a fixed-wing aircraft to the pilot.

'It's also got a heading hold, and that just works all the time. So you roll out on to a heading and it just holds it for you. And the same with the nose; so you lift the hover, and wherever you put the nose with the pedals it will just hold the nose wherever you leave it. It's got a lot of systems in it that make it nice to fly, and it trims out well; when you've got it trimmed in the hover it generally sits where you've put

it. You can trim regular helicopters, but they tend to move around as well. The system's incredible, considering that it was designed in the 1960s.

'Another unique thing about tandem-rotor helicopters is that you can do two-wheel running landings and taxiing. You effectively put the power on with a nose-up attitude, so that the front wheels are off the ground but the rear wheels are on the ground. Because of the way that the discs work you can taxi forwards and backwards and drive around with the front

ABOVE Flying in winter conditions, the pilots must monitor the aircraft for ice build-up continually, often indicated by excessive vibrations or problems with limited power. *(PRMAVIA Collection)*

LEFT A Joint Helicopter Force (JHF) Chinook flying over the Middle Eastern desert in February 2003 as part of Operation *Telic*. *(Crown Copyright)*

the Chinook will try to overtake itself; the tail will attempt to come around to the front. This is all to do with the aerodynamic effects of the airflow over the aircraft. In the mixing unit, you have systems like pitch-trim and LCTs that are constantly giving you little inputs all the time through the flight control system, and they're correcting movements of the disc as you're doing other things. When that goes [when the AFCS fails], you lose all those little inputs. With the airflow over the airframe that gives you a little bit of a torque reaction. If you look at the rear tail there's a little bit of a bend built into it, and that's all to counteract the tiny bit of torque reaction there is. The AFCS system is built to compensate for that torque. So when you lose the AFCS you get the torque input; you put a little bit of correction into the torque, but the correction gets bigger and the airframe lurches forward. You can still fly the helicopter, but the effort just becomes really hard.

'That can be a really dangerous situation in flight, particularly if you're in cloud. You can fly the Chinook without the AFCS, but it's hard work. If you're doing 120–130 knots, and the AFCS suddenly goes off, you feel it instantly as the tail attempts to swing around. You can bring the speed down, as there's a speed at which the helicopter sits much better at AFCS-out. You wouldn't want to throw the helicopter around, and you really want to get out of cloud; the helicopter is really unstable if you're trying to fly by instruments alone without AFCS, as it's very easy to get into an unusual attitude. But when AFCS is in, the Chinook flies much more like a fixed-wing aircraft.

wheels off the ground. You can use this feature effectively if you want to parallel park, in a parking spot, and if you need to back up. It also means that you can land on pinnacles of mountains, so if you can't get the whole helicopter to touch down on to a landing site you can just put the rear wheels or the ramp on that spot and you do a thing called "floating ramp".'

The impression of the Chinook given by Flight Lieutenant Thomas is one of stability, performance and near outlandish manoeuvrability, a machine perfectly configured to respond to the complex flight demands of its tactical requirements. Yet while the Chinook is a fundamentally sound design, like many modern aircraft it needs some technological assistance to make it perform at its best. The AFCS is of particular note:

'If you turn off the AFCS, the Chinook becomes very difficult to fly – without the AFCS

'With the new Mk 6, there's a thing called Digital AFCS (DAFCS), that is incredible. It does landing profiles for you just like an autopilot. You just programme it with what profile you want it to do and the aircraft will do it for you. The Americans introduced it on Black Hawk, because they had a lot of accidents during dust landings. Whenever they've introduced the DAFCS into the Black Hawk they've had no accidents attributed to pilot error during dust landings. Human error will always creep in at some point; but they've had no failures of that system – it works! People still train to fly the Chinook manually, and they always will fly it manually, but with this system you can reduce the risk – and in today's world it's all about risk reduction.'

Power and load handling

Most pilots of fixed-wing aircraft don't have to worry too much about external loads. Of course, external ordnance, avionics, fuel and other systems can be fitted to a fast jet, and these do have an effect on performance parameters. Yet the design of these features is generally streamlined and aerodynamically efficient, built to have a minimal disruption on manoeuvrability and speed. The Chinook pilot, by contrast, has to handle external loads with

all the aerodynamic properties of a breeze block. Not only that, the loads are suspended by strops, hanging and swinging beneath the aircraft. At the same time, the Chinook's cabin might be filled with several tons of armoured vehicle or dozens of fully kitted troops.

One pilot interviewed for this book explains that in many ways the Chinook is well configured to do its Herculean tasks by virtue of '... sheer lift capability, the amount of weight it can lift in comparison to other types of helicopter. The average aircraft has about 13 tonnes of fuel, and 11.3 tons is the maximum payload for an underslung load. Internally we can go up to a maximum all-up mass of 22.7 tons total, including the weight of the aircraft itself. So dependent on fuel load, I'd say that realistically we can be carrying up to about 8.5 tonnes. The fact that you've got so much power to do the lifting is incredible. Most other helicopters you run out of space and power.

'When you're transporting underslung loads the effect on the aircraft is quite noticeable, but it's quite stable because the autopilot is strong in the way it holds. It provides stabilisation, so it'll hold whatever you put on it. It's kind of like the autopilot on an airliner, where you set your height and your speed. It reduces the oscillations [of the load], so if you take it out the aircraft wants to go all over the place and you're having constantly

to correct. When you've got it selected in it will just stabilise the whole aircraft so it doesn't wallow around – you can take your hands off the controls and it'll stay doing whatever profile it was doing. But the heavier you are, the more wallowing you do, and the more cumbersome it is. It depends on the aerodynamic nature of the load as well. So if you have something like an ISO [International Standards Organization] container ... you'll really feel the weight as you start forward, whereas if your load is smaller and denser you won't feel it as much.

'If you want to liken the Chinook to something then I'd say put a heavy rucksack on very loose straps – your body still copes with it, but it just becomes a bit more cumbersome, more wobbly. I've always equated the Chinook to a Bentley R car – it has heaps of power, it's very robust and fast, and for its size it has strong performance in terms of the ability to turn and effectively throw it around. Some of the other helicopters you might describe more in terms of a Lotus Elise. The Squirrel, for example, is a very light helicopter, but it still has quite a good amount of engine power; you can throw it around corners very quickly. The Chinook really does respond very well. When you start loading it up it becomes more like a Hilux, a very rugged truck, but still quite sporty for its size. It's like the Hilux has been pimped by Ferrari.'

ABOVE A Chinook seen refuelling at RAF Shawbury. Shawbury is home to the Defence Helicopter Flying School, providing aircrew instruction, and the Central Flying School (Helicopter). *(Crown Copyright)*

BELOW To keep stable during a hover, pilots use a 'backdrop' technique, aligning themselves with key landmark features and holding them as visual reference points. *(Crown Copyright)*

The Chinook as a 'pimped' version of the Hilux is a description found in no official RAF publicity about the helicopter, but it aptly describes what the Chinook can do. Flight Lieutenant Thomas also explains how external loads alter the flying properties of the Chinook:

'The heavier the loads, the more it affects the airframe. The heaviest thing I've ever lifted is a CVRT [Combat Vehicle Reconnaissance (Tracked) – one of a family of armoured vehicles weighing in the region of 18,000lb/8,200kg]. You can really feel that underneath the aircraft, but the aircraft just copes with it. You just do everything slower. What you find with a load like that is that you've got quite a large momentum underneath the aircraft. Loads will naturally start to swing a little bit. When you start to swing with a nine-ton load or an ISO container at five or six tons, the whole airframe starts to keep time with the load. There are things that you can do to stop that, but the AFCS will also take the swing out after a little while if you let it. And we can take three loads on the three external hooks. I've lifted a 105mm gun with a netted load and some barrels; and you can take a Range Rover with its trailer connected on two hooks and something else on the front hook. It's so diverse – and you can put stuff inside while you're handling external loads. You can have troops on board plus those three loads. You could, for example, take an artillery company with field guns and the guys who man them inside, deliver them to a spot anywhere and they can be set up and ready to go within minutes. Flying with these loads is fine, but it's hard work purely because you've got that extra weight on the aircraft. You've got to be a bit more gentle to handle the swing, and you don't want to turn too tightly, because that can induce a swing – but it's no more dangerous than regular flying.

'In the hover when attaching loads, you have to adjust things a bit. You've got a radio altimeter. Generally we use that with what we call a backdrop technique – you pick a point on the horizon and something out on the side, to use when holding the Chinook in the hovering position. Say you've got a goalpost 30m in front of you, and the white bar on that happens to be at 10ft – you keep that point in your windscreen to hold your hover position. There might be something beyond that point as well, so that you can compare the two. You use that visually and your markers to keep you over the point, plus you have the crewmen talking you down in units of measure. So they'll tell you where to go over the load and they fine-tune you. The hooker (the person attaching the load to the aircraft) will stand there with the load and his earthing tool and whatever he's going to hook on, and you're flying over the top of him. Obviously you can't see him as soon as he goes underneath. The crewmen then talk to you from the hatch; normally one crewman will be looking out the front hatch on the right. He guides you in then passes you over to the other guy over the centre hatch, and he'll then talk you on with fine units of measure. He hooks the load on, and then off you go. Everybody who goes through the OCF has to do this so that they appreciate what the downwash is like. There's a 90–100mph downwash – when the Chinook runs in over the top of you it's like being buffeted in a hurricane. Once you're directly underneath the airframe it's not so bad.

'Sometimes you have to get someone to unhook the load. Any pilot or crewman can

release the load, but you might also have to train someone else to unhook the load. If you want to fly off with the strops still attached to the aircraft, the hookers have to unhook the load themselves from the side, through this 100mph downwash. It's a really good experience, especially if your mate's flying the Chinook and you've just got out to unhook the load – you've got to have a lot of trust in him.'

Dust and debris

The previous account concerning handling loads raises an issue close to the heart of all combat helicopter pilots – dust. All helicopters, if put down on unprepared surfaces, will pull up a large cloud of dust, dirt and debris, but the sheer power of the Chinook makes it an acute issue. Not only must the pilot consider the effects of the dust on the aircraft itself, but he must also take into account its impact on the people and structures in the vicinity. Flight Lieutenant Thomas again:

'Debris can be an issue. Obviously, you've got be careful where you land. Risk, as I've said, is a huge issue. You don't want to

ABOVE An infantryman reaches up to fix a load to the Chinook's centre hook, while the pilots maintain a hover above, the radio altimeter providing precision altitude information. *(Crown Copyright)*

RIGHT A Chinook suffers copious 'brownout' during a desert landing in North Africa. The pilot's aim in such landings is to touch down just as the dust is reaching window level. *(Crown Copyright)*

RIGHT Night-vision goggles fitted to a flight helmet. NVG equipment takes practice to master, as the goggles affect depth perception significantly. *(Author)*

NIGHT FLYING

Given the near-constant requirements for Chinooks to perform low-light and night flying, especially in combat zones, the Chinook pilot has to get very familiar with flying using optical aids, principally the FLIR and night-vision display goggles, as Flight Lieutenant Kyle Thomas explains:

'The FLIR turrets we have fitted are obviously very good in low-light environments. We have a technique for flying using that at night, because that will pick up things the NVG goggles really won't in the desert. To some extent they can "see" through stuff like dust. We've got night-vision systems, and obviously night flying is a staple diet of the Chinook force, because most of the things you'd want to do would be at night. We use a thing called DNVG – display night-vision goggles: it's a little monocle that you put on, and effectively it gives you a heads-up display and loads of information. You can tailor it to what you want to be displayed, from nothing to everything, so speeds, headings, GPS course bar, time, time on target or time to a point, a little AI, a hovermeter – so wherever you look you have that information in front of you, which is an invaluable tool.'

LEFT Another view of the pilot's night-vision goggles. These are actually display night-vision goggles (DNVGs), which also present flight and navigation information in front of the pilot's vision. *(Author)*

damage people, cars or anything. We can blow things away at a high rate of knots. And even being in the hover at 50ft or 100ft, you still get downwash, so you have to be careful what you're doing. You can imagine what a hurricane does to buildings, roofs and sheds, so obviously you have to be really, really careful.

'Dust is bad. It visually impairs you and it ruins aircraft, so we have to take precautions as well on the aircraft. We have the EAPS – the particle separator – fitted to the engine. It effectively sucks everything in through little holes and spins it, which creates little vortices, and spins all the sand out to the side, which then collects. Then a fan sucks that out like a vacuum, and puts that out overboard. So you get much less sand going through the engine, if any at all. We use this in snow as well. Inside the aircraft itself there's a dust curtain set across the cockpit. This prevents dust being blown back up through the airframe and into the cockpit, which can happen. So when you're doing a dust take-off or a dust approach, it's tricky, because as soon as you put power on the ground you lose visual references. It's then like flying on instruments only. Normally when you transition you wouldn't transition in mist or cloud; you'd have visual references until you fly away. Until you've got flying speed and a positive rate of climb it's quite dangerous. The idea is that you're pulling power and you're climbing vertically, and then as you come out the top of the dust cloud you transition forward.

'Then for landings, same thing. In flight, in a dust environment, there's generally not much difference unless it's hot-and-high, when you'll have a bit less performance. Then to come into a dust-landing site, you do an approach that's set up effectively. So you know where you want to land, and you'll set up at 100ft, and bring the speed back. The idea is that when you get to the point that you want to land, you flare the helicopter and touch down with little or no forward momentum. But at that point the dust cloud moves up the cabin so that, hopefully, just as the wheels touch, the dust cloud should be at the cockpit window. As you land on, the dust envelops you, but by that time you're already on the ground.

'The Chinook powers everything in Afghanistan because it's hot-and-high.

In these conditions you've got thinner air because of the height above sea level, and because it's hot the air is also thinner. So you can't get as much air into the engines, and the air going in is warmer to start with. Airflow does have a certain cooling effect when it enters the engines, so in hot-and-high conditions your engine temperatures run hotter. So quite often you run out of power, because you're limited by the engine's performance, as your engines get to their higher temperatures quicker. And sometimes, depending on where you are, you'll be torque limited. So if you're really high you could be torque limited because you're pulling more pitch on the blades and there's more torque on the shafts, and there's less air going through the discs. Therefore the lift for the hover requires more power because you

The Chinook Display Team is a unique group within the RAF's Chinook force. It is composed of personnel from both 18 (B) and 27 Squadrons, supported by engineers from 18/27 Engineering Squadron, all based at RAF Odiham. The team regularly puts on displays at air shows and other prominent events, and is renowned for its mesmerising ability to throw these huge airframes around with astonishing precision. A list of the manoeuvres for the 2013 shows hints at the versatility of both pilots and aircraft:

- ■ 'Nose over' at the crowd.
- ■ 'See-saw'.
- ■ 360° turn.
- ■ 270 nose-down quick stop.
- ■ 'Gornji' climb.
- ■ 720 corkscrew.
- ■ Wing over.
- ■ Nose over.
- ■ Wing over.
- ■ 'Roller coaster'.
- ■ Pedal turn to running landing.
- ■ Rearward 2-wheel taxi.
- ■ Backward take-off.
- ■ Bow.
- ■ Over-the-shoulder departure.

Flight Lieutenant Kyle Thomas, the display manager for 2013, explains that the Display Team's manoeuvres leave a big impression on all who witness them, even aircrew from other countries: 'When the Chinook Display Team started, a pilot called Squadron Leader Dave Morgan decided to try out various manoeuvres, and it just grew from that into a more dynamic display every year. The display team has also made a big difference to what we can do with the aircraft. People are always amazed at the size of the helicopter and what it can do.'

Thomas also describes how the team's personnel are selected: 'Usually the display team is selected every year. People volunteer – they put their names into the hat and say that they'd like to do it, and the people are selected based on stringent qualification criteria and experience. The RAF will never actually tell anyone to take on the role, because obviously that person is giving up quite a lot of their life to do the role. You do it alongside your normal job – it's not full time. For the first days of the week you're doing your normal job, then you go away with the display team on Thursday or Friday. You get very little time off from May/June to September.'

Although the commitments of the Display Team are heavy, there is no doubt that it has had a central role in building up public and professional awareness of just what the Chinook can do.

BELOW A Chinook performs a hard bank. Directional control in the Chinook is achieved by altering the plane of rotation in the rotors. *(Crown Copyright)*

have to move more air through the disc. So if you're really high you can be torque limited, but if you're low and hot you can be engine temperature limited. If the engine gets too hot, obviously it's going to break or seize, so you have to stop at your limits. You also can't pull any more torque than you're limited to because you'll end up breaking gearboxes and shafts.'

Flying in combat

Flying the Chinook in combat naturally brings with it a whole host of extra demands, demands that can be perceived but not entirely practised in training. During an interview with the author, four pilots with extensive combat flying experience in Afghanistan were asked how training and reality matched up. Here their multiple individual responses are merged into one:

'No training environment that we use is perfectly representative of the real thing. So, for example, California is hot but it is not high. Jordan is a bit higher but not quite as hot.

'The IRT job that we do, for example. You can't train for that, even if you sit in the simulator all day. In Afghanistan you're sat around with the crew, and someone will rush in and say "You've got a job, go!" And you feel a massive adrenaline rush. In training you also can't adequately represent all the players – the ops room doing their task, air traffic being potentially busy with all the different call signs in the circuit, a tiny minor aircraft snag at the start, which might delay you for a minute or so, static on the radio, sand in the controls. You can't get the adequate realism in training, but we do come pretty close.

'The way we get around it is that when we get out to theatre, the captains will have done probably three detachments before as co-pilot, so that by the time they're flying with the more junior guys they're pretty experienced themselves. So you'd never really get a crew going out and flying together who'd never been in that environment before. And the most junior guys that go out, the guys that go out with the first detachment, fly with a training captain or an instructor – the personnel who've been around the longest, and who are the most experienced

and who've had specific training in teaching new guys. You pick up everything else when you're out there.'

The combination of realistic training (as far as possible), experienced mentoring and sheer flying hours in a war zone produces pilots with a deep understanding of the operational and theatre requirements. Yet combat flying

ABOVE This Chinook displays the Pegasus rampant symbol of 18 Squadron, with a German air force helicopter in the background. *(Crown Copyright)*

BELOW A Chinook over Afghanistan launches flares; the pilot can release flares manually, or they can be triggered automatically by the DAS (defensive aids suite) system. *(PRMAVIA Collection)*

ABOVE A flight-deck crew member guides in a Chinook helicopter on to the deck of HMS *Bulwark* during a deployment to the Mediterranean in 2012. *(Crown Copyright)*

BELOW An RAF Chinook lifts a Land Rover during Exercise Wessex Thunder on Salisbury Plain in 2012. During the exercise, Chinooks provided lift to the 2nd Battalion, the Parachute Regiment (2 PARA), working with the Omani Western Frontier Regiment from the Royal Omani Army. *(Crown Copyright)*

also brings with it levels of stress and mental pressure rarely encountered in peacetime service. How do the Chinook pilots cope with these effects? In some cases, combat flying seems to bring out a psychological strength and focus when it is most needed:

'I find that when I'm under stress – the times when I've been shot at, but still need to get the job right to save someone's life – I actually perform better and I'm less likely to miss stuff, and I think that most of the crews are the same. I think that you can place yourself on the "arousal graph". If you're just chugging around the UK, it can be a pretty boring flight, and you can potentially miss stuff because you're so under-aroused. But when you have that adrenaline coursing through your veins, I find that that extra stress level actually helps me out. The fact is that we train for war very regularly, and we train for emergencies far more regularly than airline pilots do. Every time we go into the simulator we'll have a bagful of emergencies. Fairly regularly they'll shoot at us in the simulator as well. It's not the same being shot at by pixels as it is being shot at by bullets, but we do train for it so regularly that your brain shuts down some of the emotion. But the focus part of your brain sticks with doing what it has to do. That's the other reason why we do everything in such a standardised fashion. We have standard operating procedures [SOPs] for everything we do, so every profile that we fly has a SOP, and you drill those into yourself so much that you can pretty much do them without thinking about it.'

Against this backdrop of mental management, the crews also have to deal with the issue of fatigue. Frequently, multiple operations are flown daily, and with so much responsibility resting on the pilots procedures have to be implemented to reduce the risk of human error:

'We have enough crews to swap over, so you don't just constantly fly. We also have very strict rules for how many hours you can fly in a day, how many hours' sleep you must have in between flying days. We have fatigue-monitoring systems, so we'll monitor each other more than we'll monitor ourselves. The whole detachment has tables on which we score each individual, so there might be 30 people on a detachment and I'll score each person out of ten, or whatever, and if their mean score gets up to a certain point then we'll give them a

day or two off. So fatigue is very, very carefully managed because it's such a significant risk, especially in Afghanistan where we do so much more flying than we do here.'

Confidence in the Chinook

The Chinook pilots and crews fly a varied range of operations. While some of these operations are undoubtedly dramatic – such as IRT or troop insertions – a large percentage of sorties are flown for more mundane but just as essential purposes:

'We do a lot of what the Americans call "Ass and Trash", hauling blokes, bergens, mail. We were out before Christmas last year and we were shifting five tons of mail every day. For the guys who are out in the PBs and out in the FOBs, the only way to get supplies to them is by helicopter. So everything that goes into that FOB, or comes out of that FOB, must do so in the back on a Chinook or another helicopter type. The ration packs are much, much better than they used to be, but if the guys are on "rat packs" for eight, nine, ten days, then just to fly in with a box of apples or a box of bananas improves morale so much. So the majority of the work we do out there is shifting "Ass and Trash" around.'

Regardless of what mission the pilots fly, however, the fact remains that for a new generation of pilots Afghanistan and Iraq have provided a high-pressure test environment for the Chinook. In Afghanistan, a key challenge for any aircraft is to cope with the 'hot-and-high' conditions, and in this respect the Chinook hasn't been found wanting:

'We had an engine upgrade about three years ago, to what they call 714 engines, which in this country and many other environments doesn't make a huge amount of difference. The limit that you work to is a transmission torque limit. Then as you get higher and hotter, and the air gets thinner, the engines are working harder and harder. At a certain point you're

ABOVE The Apache is the Chinook's guardian angel in Afghanistan. Insurgent attempts to fire on the Chinook will usually be subdued in the presence of a hunting Apache. *(PRMAVIA Collection)*

LEFT The Chinook is a welcome sight for ground troops. Here RAF Benson Puma Force soldiers wait for the Chinook at the Bramley training area during Exercise Tigerheart, 2013. *(Crown Copyright)*

Chinook pilots must learn to handle the most unusual loads, in this case a Royal Marine rigid-inflatable boat (RIB), during an 'underslinging' insertion of waterborne personnel. *(Crown Copyright)*

ABOVE **This amazing display of flying shows how precisely the Chinook can maintain a hover, as the 'hookers' attach loads to all three hook points.** *(Crown Copyright)*

BELOW **A camouflaged Chinook is guided in to pick up a load. The crewman at the door provides visual references to the pilots at the front.** *(Crown Copyright)*

maxing out the engines, and working them as hot as they can possibly work, and you're not quite achieving that maximum torque limit on the transmission. So when it's cold you'll always reach the transmission limit before the engine limit, whereas when it's hot-and-high you'll be engine limited.

'In Afghanistan we used to be engine limited way before we got to the transmission limit with the old system. In the middle of summer you're looking at 50+°C [122°F] and 3,000ft [914m] altitude at Camp Bastion. But with the new upgrade, even in the height of summer we're now getting to the point where it's very close whether you're transmission limited or engine limited. In the really hot periods it's given us a much greater lift capability, meaning that we really don't have to reduce the number of passengers or weight of loads that we fly at any point during the year. Some of the helicopter types that have been out there have been able to carry quite a few passengers during the winter. The Merlin, for example, can fly 24 people in the winter, but that drops down to about 8 in the summer. So they vary hugely in what they can carry seasonally, but we tend not to have that problem.'

The pilots were also keen to point out that there has been some misunderstanding about the nature of the terrain over which they operate in Afghanistan:

'A lot of people confuse the operation we've been involved in in Afghanistan with mountainous terrain. Really, most of the stuff we've been involved in over Afghanistan has been over flat desert and small populated areas. There are some small mountains in the British standard area of operations [AoR] in Afghanistan, but they're not really that big and we don't spend a lot of time in them.

'The way that that environment becomes more difficult is because the place where Camp Bastion and Kandahar sit is about 3,000ft [914m] above sea level, whereas RAF

TOP Two Chinooks fly in formation. Both are fitted with external rescue hoists, but the furthest Chinook also has the forward-looking infrared (FLIR) turret beneath the nose. *(Crown Copyright)*

ABOVE This fine photograph of a Chinook shows the port side to good effect. Features include the aerial 'ladder' down the side plus chaff and flare boxes on the lower rear fuselage. *(Crown Copyright)*

BELOW A Chinook taxis along the runway at Odiham, the front rotor angled forward via the cyclic to give forward movement. *(Crown Copyright)*

Odiham is 405ft [123m] above sea level, and Afghanistan is a lot hotter in summer. The times when we do go up to the mountains tend to be when we're supporting other nationalities. We've done a lot of stuff with Norwegian guys and the American forces up in the mountains, whereas the AoR in which the Brits are working tends to be the green zone of Helmand, which is all within about 3 miles [1.8km] of a river, and fairly low.'

One area in which all the pilots concur is that the Chinook offers impressive survivability for the high-risk situations into which they fly. A key reason given for this is the duplication of major systems, such as engines, hydraulics and electrical systems.

'When the Americans designed this aircraft they pretty much designed it to take an awful lot of punishment on the battlefield. The way they designed it, the hydraulic systems are separated – you've got one at the front of the aircraft and one at the back. Major systems are separated so that if you do take damage in one area of the aircraft you don't lose it all, whereas in other helicopters everything important tends to be grouped up together.

'The whole thing's been designed as a battlefield helicopter from the floor up. Some helicopters are designed as civilian helicopters and are then militarised. The Chinook was designed just before the Vietnam conflict, so it's been pretty well tested in combat.

'The blades are also key to the helicopter's reliability. The blades can have a chunk taken out of them and the helicopter won't fall out of the sky immediately, unlike many other helicopters. It's quite a simple blade actually, and you can take bullet holes through them and you'll experience a bit of vibration but ultimately you can keep going.'

Changing views

Visiting Odiham as an outsider, the understated pride of the crews and all those on the base is palpable. In an era in which defence spending is frequently threatened, and with a growing gravitation towards unmanned aerial vehicles (UAVs) in many areas of fixed-wing aviation, the RAF Chinook force remains utterly contemporary and totally relevant to

modern warfare. Those who man the Chinook have therefore found themselves more in the media spotlight, whereas previously they lived more under the shadow of the jet's wing.

One pilot observed: 'Most people of my era probably joined the air force to fly fast jets. But once people are in the rotary world, the Chinook world, this is the place to be. I think it's changing, because if you speak to a lot of the air cadets who we see, with the amount of press coverage and action that the Chinooks have seen, specifically in Afghanistan, it has changed that view a little bit. A lot of youngsters now want to fly helicopters as their first choice.'

The high visibility of the Chinook is warranted and timely. The men and women who pilot this remarkable aircraft perform tasks that deserve recognition. As we have seen in this chapter, the Chinook represents a successful marriage of human and machine in an operational context, and as such the Chinook and its pilots are likely to grace our screens and newspapers for many years to come.

ABOVE Two Chinooks in formation flight at Odiham. As well as three Support Helicopter (SH) squadrons, Odiham houses one Army Air Corps (AAC) Lynx squadron. *(Crown Copyright)*

BELOW The HC-2 cockpit, showing the centre instrument panel, the canted console and the pilot's and co-pilot's instrument panels. *(Crown Copyright)*

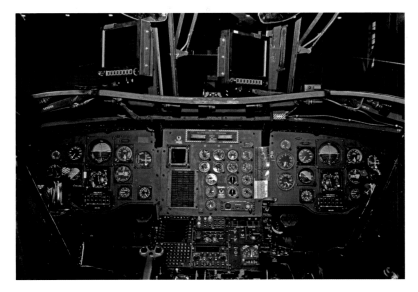

Chapter Six

The crew's view

The Chinook is a crew-manned aircraft, and each of the four personnel on board is essential to the tactical and logistical efficiency of the helicopter. The two weapons support operators (WSOps – known as Crewmen) in the back, like the pilots up front, share the dangers of front-line service, while also performing a unique and demanding set of roles.

OPPOSITE **The WSOs must manage both personnel and vehicles aboard the Chinook, ensuring that any heavy equipment is anchored firmly and weapons/ammunition are in the safest positions.** *(Crown Copyright)*

In 2013, Sergeant Anna Irwin, a Chinook
WSOp on the immediate response team from
18 Squadron at Camp Bastion, Afghanistan,
received the dreaded emergency call. A Taliban
suicide bomber had detonated a bomb at a UK
patrol base in Helmand Province, the explosion
inflicting multiple casualties. Within minutes,
Irwin and the rest of the crew were airborne,
and it soon became clear that they were flying
into a 'hot' landing zone: 'Once airborne, we
could see a big plume of smoke. We were told
casualty numbers were changing and I sensed
there was a big incident. We landed on our
second approach and lowered the ramp. I saw
more and more people coming through the
fog. The medic went out to triage and the RAF
Regiment lads went out to give protection. It
was chaotic, there was loads of firing.'

Soon the casualties were flooding aboard
the aircraft, Irwin having to work hard to attend
to the casualties while also updating the pilot
on the situation around. The Chinook and the
surrounding British troops were under fire all
around from small arms and RPGs: 'I've been
in lots of situations, but never been under so
much fire before. When I was off the cab, there
was a massive explosion and it shook the cab
and I felt it through my body, in my chest. It's
for me to keep the crew informed that we still
have guys off the back of the ramp, that we're
still working with the casualties, and to reassure
them that the aircraft is OK, even though they
can see bullets splashing around.'

Keeping her focus, Irwin went about ensuring
that everyone was safely on board, then
informed the pilot that it was now safe to take

off. As the helicopter lifted off, enemy fire came
in from all sides. In response, Irwin grabbed the
M60 machine gun mounted on the rear ramp,
and sprayed the enemy positions with 7.62mm
fire.

For this act of composure under fire,
Sergeant Anna Irwin was given the award of
Most Outstanding Airman at the December
2013 Military Awards ceremony, the
presentation by HRH the Prince of Wales and
the Duchess of Cornwall. Yet looking beyond
the award given, there is much about the
action of Sergeant Irwin that speaks volumes
about the experience of the Chinook's WSOps.
First, despite being aircrew, those who man
the Chinook can be just as close to front-line
infantry combat as the soldiers on the ground.
The entire Chinook and its crew were, during
this action, directly in the enemy line of fire,
taking both small-arms and RPG rounds.
Second, operating the Chinook in combat is
evidently a crew matter, the WSOps interacting
with numerous other individuals – ground
troops, medical team and pilots. The actions of
people like Anna Irwin have been repeated on
hundreds of occasions over the last 13 years
(at the time of writing) in Afghanistan and other
theatres, and they attest to the near-unique job
the WSOps perform within the Royal Air Force.

Roles and duties

Up until recent years, the main job title for a
crewman aboard a Chinook (or any other
RAF helicopter for that matter) was 'loadmaster'.
The description in many ways conveyed
the reality of the crewman's role, but it was
subsequently changed to the more technical
'weapons support operator' (WSOp). The full
title for a Chinook crewman, therefore, would
be 'weapons support operator (crewman)'.
Although the title shifts the focus to the weapon-
handling role, which in reality forms a minor
part of the crewman's duties, the loadmaster
functions are embedded within the role.

The personnel in the Chinook's cabin also
have a distinction between them of being
No 1 and No 2 crewmen. Here is where the
full spectrum of Chinook WSOp responsibilities
emerge, and a job that requires extremely high
levels of training and technical acumen:

Here the training route for a weapons support operator is explained by a Chinook WSOp:

'You start off at the same selection course that the pilots attend – the Officers and Aircrew Selection Centre (OASC) at RAF Cranwell in Lincolnshire – where you do some aptitude, fitness and leadership tests over a four-day selection course. If you're successful you get a letter telling you that they'd like you to come back. You go back and do a Part 2 medical, which involves some extra tests they didn't do in the initial medical. Then the first part of the course is a ten-week leadership course at RAF Cranwell for non-commissioned aircrew. If you pass that stage you move on to 45(R) Squadron at RAF Cranwell, where you do around six months of aviation classes. At this point we're all generic WSOps, so we have to be streamed into various different roles – helicopters, fixed-wing, sensor. For helicopter guys the next stage in the training would be to go down to RAF Shawbury, near Shrewsbury in Shropshire, where you'd do a year-long course. You'd begin your full training on the Bell 412, which is like the Huey but with an extra set of blades on top, so you've got four blades instead of two. You do your flying training on there, and when you've qualified you get streamed to a specific aircraft type: Chinook, Merlin or Puma. We join the pilots on their sorties; you normally have a student pilot in the front with an instructor, and a student crewman in the back with a crewman instructor. We wouldn't go into the front of the aircraft – we stay in the rear – but we still learn navigation and many technical aspects of flying. After that you'd go to an Operational Conversion Flight (OCF) and then on to a squadron.'

Sergeant Kevin Robertson, an experienced WSOp in 27 Squadron, here clarifies more about the types of duties involved in being a Chinook crewman:

'The primary thing for helicopter crewmen would be voice marshalling. The pilots don't always have good eyes beneath the aircraft, particularly when we're trying to negotiate our way into tight landing zones – which we call "confined areas". The pilot is sat at the front, but obviously behind him he's got another 100ft of aircraft. It's quite handy for the pilot to have our eyes at the back providing him descriptions of things like how far we are from the ground, and we give them a countdown of that. The Chinook is quite capable, so we've got three big hooks under the aircraft for underslung loads. Obviously the pilot can't see underneath to negotiate getting those hooked on using a hooking team, so we'd guide him with voice marshalling with instructions such as "forward, back, up, down, left, right," just to get him into exactly the right position.

'Every other role is focused inside the cabin: looking after the passengers, ensuring that they're secure, instructing them how to exit the aircraft safely in an emergency, strapping down all their kit so that any baggage that comes aboard with them is secure (in the event of a crash, we don't want it flying about all over the place). We can get things like Land Rovers and other wheeled vehicles into the back of the aircraft. Each vehicle comes with a scheme that dictates how they need to be strapped into the aircraft, because obviously you don't want to break any major components on the vehicle when it's strapped down, but you also want to make sure that it's secure. This is where the loadmaster role comes into our jobs. There are quite a lot of rules and regulations which govern this role, so you become the subject matter expert on the captain's behalf when it comes to loading things.'

BELOW A crewman leans over the ramp of the Chinook, communicating to the pilots about hazards and giving approximate altitude as the aircraft comes in to land. *(Crown Copyright)*

BELOW A Chinook No 1 crewman looks out of the back of a Chinook during an exercise over the North African desert in 2009, providing voice marshalling to the pilots. *(Crown Copyright)*

ABOVE A crewman stands in the starboard door of a Chinook; the upper part of the door (which features a jettisonable window) slides into the cabin on tracks, secured in place by a latch. *(Crown Copyright)*

ABOVE The helicopter winch grip. Note the cable cutter button, which when initiated fires a ballistic cartridge for instantaneous severing of the winch cable and its load. *(Crown Copyright)*

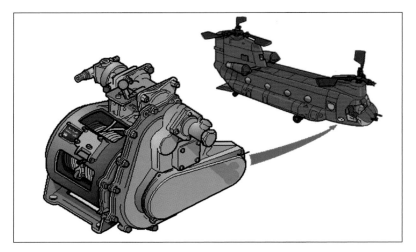

LEFT A diagram showing the location of the Chinook's internal winch; its location allows powered cargo loading to be applied for the full length of the cabin floor. *(Crown Copyright)*

'The No. 2 crewman is up at the front of the aircraft between the pilots, so his role is more about navigation assist, or he can take the navigation fully. With the Mk 4s, 5s and 6s that are coming in, the No 2 has a moving map in front of him, just like the pilots have at the front, so the No 2 can and does take sole navigation duties, which allow the left-hand seat pilot [in the cockpit] to concentrate more on things like night-time forward-looking infrared, sorting out his next radio frequencies etc. So in essence the No 2's role is pilot assist. If we had a large tasking sheet the No 2 crewman would have the tasking sheet and would be constantly reminding the captain of what the next role was going to be and the best way to do it.

LEFT An RAF ground crew member hooks up a load. Out of shot, another serviceman reaches forward with an earthing hook to release the build-up of static electricity charge from the coupling to the ground *(Crown Copyright)*

'The No 1 crewman is much more in charge of the loading scheme and the cabin, so if there was a large loading of vehicles and packs he would choose the best way to arrange that. Also, in the cabin we have a maintenance panel. It's quite old-fashioned, but it displays your hydraulic temperatures and pressures, and it's got latches for all the oil systems that tell you if you've picked up any metal substance in there. They're latched to bring attention to the No 1 crewman, so he can alert the rest of the crew if there's possibly a problem with the gearboxes or engines.'

Note that while the crewmen might be assigned to No 1 or No 2 roles for a specific mission, they will frequently swap their roles between missions, both to stave off complacency and to keep hard-learned skills fresh.

Managing loads

As the pilot accounts indicated in the previous chapter, much of what the Chinook does are 'Ass and Trash' missions, carrying cargo and personnel around the theatre. Cargo can obviously go either into the cabin itself or be carried as an underslung load. If the latter is to be acquired, high levels of cooperation are required between the ground forces, the crewmen and the pilots, as Sergeant Robertson again explains:

'Standard procedure for picking up an underslung load would first start with a functional check on the hooks, to make sure that they all work. In training we have a Tac Park – Tactical Park – at Odiham, which is run by a team of ground-support personnel who do the actual hooking up on to the aircraft, although we can do it ourselves sometimes, depending on what we're loading. We would get ourselves down to the Tac Park, and we've got a centre hatch in the floor in the cabin which we open up. Across the main beam you have the centre hook, which can take up to 11.3 tons (11,300kg) of weight on it. There are obviously two crewmen in the rear of the cabin. The crewman at the front will get the aircraft going in the right general direction [via voice marshalling] and into the general overhead location of the load.

'The No 2 crewman is at the starboard door, and he has a lookout arc from the one o'clock

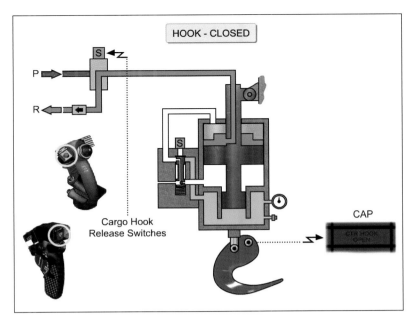

ABOVE The hook operating system, showing how an internal piston powers the hook action. Note the two cargo release switches: one on a handle in the cabin, the other on the collectives. *(Crown Copyright)*

LEFT The external rescue hoist mounted over the starboard door of the Chinook, used for light personnel and small cargo lifts. Not all Chinooks receive the hoist as a standard fitment. *(Crown Copyright)*

LEFT A Chinook crewman leans out of the starboard door onboard HMS *Bulwark*, during the ship's deployment to the Mediterranean in 2012. *(Crown Copyright)*

around to the five o'clock. The No 1 crewman operates from near the ramp, looking out to the left, so his lookout arc is from the six o'clock all the way around to the ten o'clock. The No 2 crewman will get the aircraft to the overhead position above the load, and then they'll do fine-tuning with their voice marshalling to get the hook right over the hooker-up's position – there'll be a person on the ground ready to attach the load to the hook. [Within the armed services, regular courses are run for ground troops to train them in the technicalities and procedures of hooking-up, so the Chinook's crew can usually rely on trained personnel down below.] Once that's done you'll negotiate lifting

that up and taking it elsewhere.

'The aircraft can discharge its own static via a little static line on the aft left wheel; however, if the helicopter isn't going to land on there's lots of static charge built up and ready to go. We discharge this with a little earthing lead, which should be in contact with the ground before attaching the load to the metal hook. We have something called a "light line", which we can attach to the far end of the strop, and that's just to save us having to pull the strop in by hand – we can pull the little bit of rope up and recover the heavy-duty strop without having to land on.

'As well as using strops, the crew can also take on loads using the "shepherd's crook" – a metal rod that looks a little like an actual shepherd's crook. We use that if we don't have any hooking team, and it means that the loads can be picked up by the aircrew itself. [When using this] the No 1 crewman will have his head right into the hatch with the shepherd's crook and when we get to the load he'll make sure that the helicopter stays stable, using voice marshalling, and he'll use the shepherd's crook to snare the eye of the shackle, lift up the shackle and hook it on to the aircraft itself.'

The process for taking aboard vehicles is naturally quite different. Here the focus is on ensuring that the vehicle is secured within the Chinook in a regulated manner:

'To load vehicles into the cabin, we put the ramp down and make sure that we've got enough clearance. There are loading schemes for all the vehicles that could sit inside the rear, so ideally before a vehicle comes on board you'll have had a big document out beforehand, and you'll know all about it. The document gives the exact tie-down points and the exact piece of equipment you need to safely manage that vehicle and get it strapped down. You land on and put the ramp down, and we've got toe ramps [extensions], and they're put down to allow us to get wheeled and tracked vehicles inside. The No 1 crewman will remain on the ramp and the No 2 crewman will probably go out and help marshal the vehicle into the cabin without touching the sides of the helicopter. Once the vehicle is in, you follow the loadscheme that's been laid out for you to secure that vehicle to the floor. You can also use the internal winch to haul vehicles into the aircraft.'

ABOVE Soldiers from the 7 Armoured Brigade (the Desert Rats) attended a course held at Princess Royal Barracks Gutersloh in March 2012, to learn how to attach cargo to a Chinook helicopter. *(Crown Copyright)*

BELOW A Chinook is refuelled in a remote location. With additional fuel tanks installed internally in the cabin, the Chinook itself can serve as a refuelling point using the FARE system. *(Crown Copyright)*

Weapons handling

In hostile areas, the Chinook is frequently armed to give it a significant defensive capability. Two types of weapon are traditionally mounted: the M60 machine gun and the M134 Minigun. The M60 is an adapted 7.62mm belt-fed infantry weapon, typically mounted to the Chinook on the ramp area. While the M60 fires at a cyclic rate of about 550rpm, the M134 Minigun, an electrically powered rotary barrel weapon of incredible firepower, fires at a rate of 3,000 rpm. The Minigun is used to deliver heavy defensive fire, and the Chinook can mount two such weapons: one at the starboard door and one at the port window. They have been modified for the Chinook so

that they don't actually need the aircraft power system to operate, which means they can still be used if the aircraft goes down with complete power failure and is under attack. The guns are powered by 12V DC batteries, which can be charged from the aircraft. The Minigun's magazine canister can hold up to 4,000 rounds, although typically it is only loaded up to about 3,800 rounds. The battery will have enough power to empty about 12 of those boxes. The empty cases are ejected via a tube outside the aircraft, and the guns are fitted with various physical stops to prevent the gunner shooting bits off his own aircraft.

Obviously training is required for the WSOps to use these systems effectively in combat. Sergeant Robertson elucidates:

'We essentially do the same weapons training as any other person in the ground forces would, so we also do rifle and pistol drills every six months to make sure that we're current on those. We're taught aerial firing techniques. The speed of the aircraft is obviously carried on to the round that leaves the aircraft – so you have to lead the target, so that the rounds fall in the right location. It sounds quite difficult, but because the weapon [the M134] has such a high rate of fire, and because one in every four rounds we fire is a tracer round, you see what looks like a broken line of light leaving the weapon, and you can observe your fall of shot very easily and correct it very accurately.'

The bullets in flight are influenced by the forces of the helicopter's airflow on the rounds, and the way that the round spins, so the aiming point requires adjustment depending on which side of the cabin the gun is mounted:

'Our weapons are all rifled to a clockwise spin [on the bullet]. So when you fire out of the starboard door, and the bullet is spinning in a clockwise direction, the airflow is hitting the bullet from the left-hand side. The impact of the airflow causes the round to spin down. So from the right-hand door you're leading the target from behind it and up. We have an expression to remember this: "Fire to the right – right right high". So if you're firing from the right of the aircraft, you have to aim to the right side of the target – which would be behind it – and high. From the left-hand side, the round is spinning in a clockwise direction and into the airflow, but this time the airflow will cause the round to move up [elevate]. So from this side of the target the expression is "Fire to the left – left left low" [firing from the left, aim to the left, again behind the target, but lower the aim to compensate for the upward drift of the bullets into the airflow]. The M60, however, which is only fitted to the ramp, is a little bit more straightforward [because the gunner is shooting directly out of the back, rather than into a slipstream crosswind].'

Mastering the weapons takes practice, but as our opening account of Anna Irwin indicates,

ABOVE A crewman's SA80 rifle stowage system. All crewmen must be prepared for the eventuality of ground engagements, should the aircraft be downed in hostile areas. *(Crown Copyright)*

the WSOps can make a direct firepower contribution on the battlefield, protecting themselves and all those aboard.

BELOW LEFT As an alternative to the Minigun, the 7.62mm L7A2 general-purpose machine gun can also be pintle-mounted to the side door of the Chinook, to provide suppressing fire. *(Crown Copyright)*

BELOW The Minigun has a 4,000rpm rate of fire. The gun is electrically powered by an independently chargeable DC battery, which can sustain fire even when the aircraft is powered down. *(Crown Copyright)*

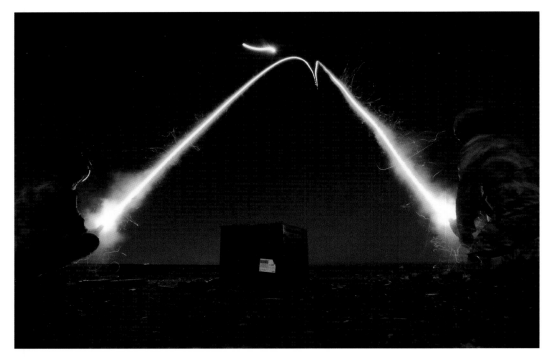

Operations

In interview with a WSOp, the author asked a similar question to that posed to the pilots in the previous chapter: how much does training prepare for the real experience of operations? Naturally the nature of that experience depends much on the character of the person involved. Some individuals experience combat with surges of adrenaline, while others experience

a heightened awareness but might even feel a sense of calm or control. The WSOp agreed, however, that good training was vital, but it could only take you so far:

'There are some things that you can't possibly train for, and there are things you need to see yourself before you can learn them. But the Chinook is such a versatile beast that we can do almost everything in it, so we train for such a variety of roles that we can never really cover one thing in too much depth. Obviously, in Afghanistan we encounter situations that you can't prepare for. For example, in extremis and as dictated by the ground situation, we can have an aircraft that's so full that you can't see from front to back because of bags and personnel – you'd never practise that in the UK, because it's probably not the safest thing to do, but under the circumstances in Afghanistan it's what you needed to do at the time. Generally I really enjoy going on operations and working this aircraft.

'Our role in the IRT relates to the aircraft only. We get the aircraft there as quickly as we can, obviously looking after the safety of the medics and the force protection that we have on board. We do receive some medical training, but we're not the experts in there, so we don't get involved with that on board unless the situation dictates. We obviously can't train for what sights you might see. Before you go away to Afghanistan,

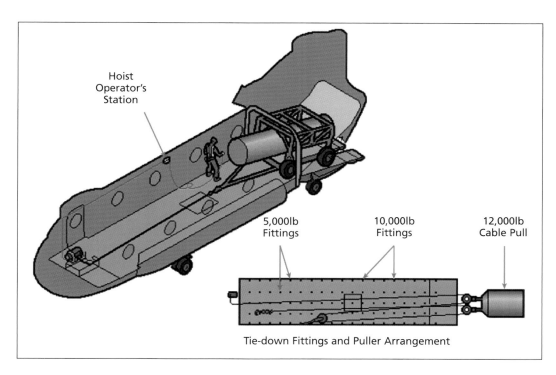

Hoist
Operator's
Station

5,000lb
Fittings

10,000lb
Fittings

12,000lb
Cable Pull

Tie-down Fittings and Puller Arrangement

LEFT A diagram showing the arrangement of the internal hoist aboard the Chinook, plus the cabin floor tie-down fittings. The hoist operator's station is set forward, so the crewman can monitor the load as it is pulled on board. *(Crown Copyright)*

however, the experienced guys will share their stories and expertise.'

As with the pilots, however, the WSOps take comfort from the presence of an Apache guardian:

'When we're going into hostile areas we normally have an escort. In previous times this would be a Lynx, which would have a .50-cal or a GPMG [general-purpose machine gun] fitted, but now we tend to have an Apache. In hostile areas we pick up ICOM chatter between the Taliban forces on the ground, so you're generally aware if they can see you and when you're moving into hostile areas. You have intelligence briefings before you fly out, and rely on previous experience, so you generally know when you're going somewhere that's hostile, but generally the hostiles aren't too interested in playing with you if you have an Apache along with you. They've got used to that, and so they're very, very clever and very flexible in their own tactics.'

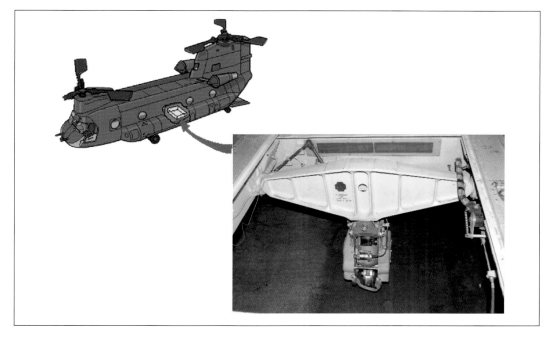

LEFT The centre hatch of the Chinook; the photo shows the main T-beam – the strongest part of the aircraft – from which the centre hook hangs. *(Crown Copyright)*

ABOVE A Chinook picks up a large netted load. The frontal crewman will have already directed the pilots over the loads, avoiding nearby obstacles such as the trees on the left.
(Crown Copyright)

On the Chinook

The Chinook is without doubt a demanding workspace for the WSOps. The sheer range of duties they have to perform requires not only a technical mindset but also excellent leadership and people management skills. As to the experience of flight itself, the WSOps have to develop at the least a strong sense of balance and an absolute immunity to air sickness. Although a pilot, Kyle Thomas of the Chinook Display Team recognises that the people at the back need to be made of stern stuff, while also following relevant safety procedures:

'The most Gs you'll pull in the display team is about 2–3, but that's only for a very short time. It's not sustained like in a fixed wing or a jet, where when you pull it on and it's there the whole time you're pulling. It's worse down the back, especially if you're a crewman standing up. Think about it … if you're stood at the back on the ramp and you've got 100ft of aircraft turning around the nose, that's quite a huge circumference. It's quite a force. The crew in the rear have a monkey-tail harness which they clip on to different rings. They adjust their straps depending on what position they're in in the cabin, so that they can lean out the door but won't fall out. As they move around they just unclip and then clip on again, wherever they need to be.'

Yet despite the noise, cold and violent movements, most Chinook WSOps demonstrate a commitment and loyalty to the Chinook. It offers a space quite different from any other airframe, and a team community that is purposeful and cooperative. Sergeant Robertson has the final say on his affection for the Chinook:

'The Chinook is spacious, which you can't say for many helicopters – being able to stand up is great! I really enjoy working on the Chinook itself. Obviously the environment can be cold, especially if it's cold outside and you have to leave the door open. In Afghanistan in the middle of summer it's really, really hot on the ground, but when you get up to something like 6,000ft it's obviously quite a bit cooler up there. We generally don't go above 8,000ft, so we don't suffer from any altitude effects. There's quite a lot of vibration going on – think about sitting on top of a washing machine when the spin cycle is going! However, it's the safest helicopter you can get, so I'd much rather be in it than in anything else.'

RIGHT The WSO on board an 18 (B) Squadron Chinook helicopter embarks the MERT for another mission from Camp Bastion over Helmand Province, Afghanistan. *(Crown Copyright))*

BELOW The floor of the Chinook can take rollered runners down the centre section, to ease the loading of heavy palletised loads, which are pulled on board by the internal hoist. *(Crown Copyright)*

BELOW The M60 in situ on the rear ramp. The gun is set on a pintle mount that allows free traverse; note the regular bipod legs folded up beneath the muzzle. *(Crown Copyright)*

Chapter Seven

The engineer's view

The Chinook engineers are the people who keep what is arguably the RAF's most important air asset serviceable and flying. Like the aircrew, they are also a breed apart, the operational requirements of the Chinook making almost unique demands in the world of military aviation.

OPPOSITE Two Royal Air Force technicians service the rotor hub of a Chinook helicopter in the Middle East. Note the integral work platform built into the pylon. *(Crown Copyright)*

The Chinook world

In the world of RAF engineering, the distinction between rotary- and fixed-wing engineers can be pronounced. On one level, they all have to do the same things – keep the aircraft serviceable, repair it when it is broken and fit it out for role-specific tasks. Yet for the rotary-wing engineers, the environment in which they operate, and the engineering burdens that environment brings, mean that maintaining the Chinook demands far more than just engineering talent.

In an interview at RAF Odiham, the author spoke with six Chinook engineers, and while they never for a second decried the work of fixed-wing engineers (most had worked on fixed-wing aircraft in the past), they were very aware of the differences between the two worlds, as Sergeant Chris Collinson remarked:

'I've worked on training aircraft, Nimrods, Jaguars, Hawks, all sorts of things, but coming into the helicopter world is very different. The ethos is different, and the mentality of the guys working on them. One of the primary differences between us and, say, a fast-jet squadron is that quite often when a fast-jet squadron deploys, they go as a whole unit. They'll go to a fixed location, say an airbase, and, although they're in a different country, the environment will seem very similar ... everything around them will be very recognisable. For us, however, we could end up anywhere. On one particular detachment we could start off from an airbase that we recognise, then end up on the back of a ship (and there's a whole set of operations for working on the ship), and then from the ship you may move across to somewhere like Norway, where you encounter all the issues you would in the Arctic.

'Sometimes we work out of fixed sites – we might have a Portakabin available or some other fixed building. But we often operate as a smaller group, and I suppose this is why we're different. The squadron can send two aircraft and, say, a dozen engineers, but you'll take all your kit, food, accommodation and pack it all into the same aircraft that you're servicing, fly away to your new location, and then you unpack it, you set the site up, you start flying, and you basically support yourselves.

'There's a distinction between the "green" air force (that's not just Chinooks, it's the Puma guys as well), and the rest of the "blue" air force. Once you're inside the helicopter world, you either turn up and you'll stay here for a long time or you'll try to get out as quickly as

possible. Some people just can't take to it at all, they want to get back to their home comforts.

'Predominantly, if a fixed-wing aircraft has a problem it sets down at another airfield. A couple of years ago we had a Chinook that clipped a wire in Wales, but because it's a helicopter it just sits itself down in a field, and that presents quite unique problems for the engineers. We have to base ourselves out of that field in Wales. It's not an airport with all the service available.'

Here Sergeant Collinson's comments go to the heart of why the Chinook presents such challenges for its engineers. As a tactical helicopter, it is frequently forward-deployed into areas with the minimum of infrastructural support. 'With your fixed-wing aircraft,' he says, 'you need a runway, and where there's a runway there tends to be buildings, heating, a kitchen, accommodation and shelter – infrastructure, in short. With fixed-wing aviation, you have a suitcase; with rotary-wing you have a backpack.' Flight Sergeant Mark Lilley concurs with this view, and sees parallels in the past to what the Chinook engineers do today: 'You could be living in a tent, in bivi bags or even sleeping in the aircraft. If you look back to World War Two, the 2nd Tactical Air Force had the Servicing Commandos, and really we're a little bit less than that but not far off. On the battlefield we're deployed forward, operating very close to the front line and even beyond. That's not normal for a regular RAF engineer, to be outside the wire.'

The fact that Chinook engineers could go 'outside the wire' means that they often receive special tactical training, so that they can cooperate effectively with ground forces in high-risk areas. In-theatre, a force protection unit might also be assigned to the engineers, to provide perimeter security while the engineers are working on a helicopter.

Another consideration for the engineers is the need for rapid response. As Chapter Four illustrated, the versatility of the Chinook

ABOVE Fitting skis to the Chinook is a good way to prevent serious damage to the landing gear from unseen objects beneath the unbroken snow. *(PRMAVIA Collection)*

BELOW The tents by the side of this Chinook in Afghanistan can be typical accommodation for Chinook engineers, who tend to be deployed well forward in the theatre. *(Simon Wheeler)*

ABOVE Chinook engineers have to work in all manner of exposed conditions. In sub-zero temperatures, the engineering teams will often work in 10–15-minute rotations. *(PRMAVIA Collection)*

a go bag packed and ready to go. We also have a logistic section up at the top of the road, and they've got toolkits all on standby, all the tents, all the heaters, all the cookers. ... What you tend to do is just eat "rat packs" for a couple of days. I deployed to Kosovo in 1999 – by Friday evening I was in Bosnia and by Saturday morning I was in Kosovo itself. So the deployment process can be extremely quick. We used to have our own separate squadrons, and they used to keep their own kit, but everything is centralised now. The last [deployment] I did was 16 hours from the balloon going up to getting out the door. But that was mostly spent completely re-roling the cab.'

Chris Collinson agrees: 'The demands can be so wide-ranging. Both myself and Jamie [Sergeant Jamie Pearce] had a similar experience with Sierra Leone. Before we knew it – bang! – we were there. Roll forward a few years on from that, to the earthquakes in Pakistan. Before I knew it, we were on a C-17 out of Fairford destined for Islamabad and straight into the middle of Pakistan, building aircraft for earthquake relief.'

Naturally, unpredictable and frequent disruptions play havoc with the social and family life of engineers. For this reason, as Sergeant Pearce recounts, 'You normally get a period when you're on standby, which they try to work into the actual shift patterns these days. If you're back in the UK for a certain period you'll be on standby for a month, so within that period you'll know that you could potentially go here, there and everywhere. You're relatively safe unless something big occurs.'

In addition to unexpected deployments, the engineers will also have scheduled deployments, such as exercises or tours abroad. The result is that for most Chinook engineers, a significant portion of their year is spent away from Odiham.

BELOW The engineers will often configure a cabin for its specific role. Here we see a diagram of the seating plan for personnel, including central aisle seating. *(Crown Copyright)*

means that it can receive orders for rapid deployment with little notice, perhaps to fulfil an urgent overseas military requirement or to support a humanitarian relief operation. Thus like the aircrew, the engineers have to be able to deploy with everything they need within hours of a notification. Not only does this mean their own personal items, but also all the respective engineering equipment (spares, tools, computers etc) they need to maintain the aircraft in the new location. Chief Technician Simon Wheeler: 'Everybody has

Maintenance

Whatever the theatre or conditions in which the Chinook engineers find themselves, their commitment is to keep the Chinooks under their responsibility flying and meeting their required taskings. Given the level of usage demanded of the Chinooks, few aircraft are

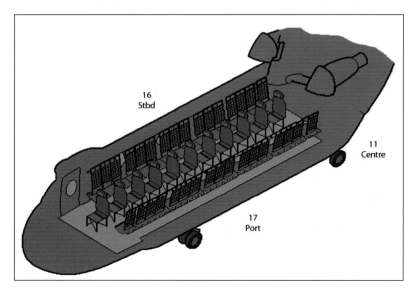

16
Stbd

11
Centre

17
Port

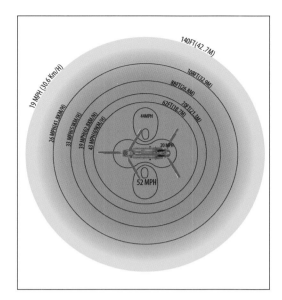

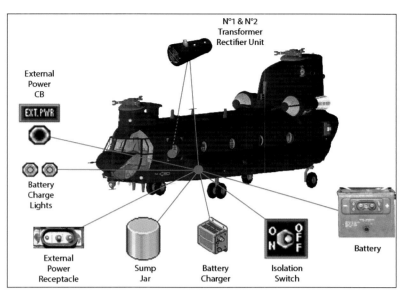

ever left standing idle, as Mark Lilley points out: 'There's a lot of pressure on the engineers to maintain serviceable aircraft out on the flightline. As soon as they're serviceable on the flightline they're being flown. The whole system is running hot. To maintain the crew levels and maintain competencies for the crews flying in Afghanistan, this station [Odiham] is running to capacity. We're limited on the number of airframes, and the training programme is intense.'

The engineering efforts at Odiham have been through several streamlining processes to achieve dramatic efficiency improvements over recent years. Up to the mid-2000s the engineering support to 18 and 27 Squadrons was provided by the unit-specific engineering personnel, but these separate units were subsequently amalgamated into a single unit of some 300 personnel. This, and other rationalisations, has brought increases in flying time in the region of tens of thousands of hours to the RAF's Chinook fleet over the years.

On a daily basis, the principal servicing requirements for the Chinook consist of Before Flight Servicing (BFS) and After Flight Servicing (AFS). The former is explained by Sergeant Collinson: 'Every day before the aircraft goes flying, the mechanics – usually the most junior members of the organisation – have to go out and perform Flightline Servicing. Normally the first servicing that they have to perform is called a Before Flight Servicing. It's normally two guys, who go out to the aircraft – one

guy upstairs, and the other guy downstairs – essentially to check in the first instance that everything's in the right place. They also check for things like hydraulic fluids at the correct levels, the pressures of the accumulators and fuel level (the fuel level will be at a specific level, and the aircrew might ask for more fuel depending on the mission). The engineers also have to see to various role requirements – for example, the aircrew might want to take more strops with them; if they're taking more troops on board, they might want more seat belts, or they may want extra nets, different lighting capabilities, etc.'

Matt Baker continues by explaining the AFS: 'The aircraft has to have a valid aircraft servicing on it, so as well as the BFS we'll also do an After Fight Servicing once it lands, or a "Turnround", which means it can go flying again, whatever that next sortie is. If the helicopter isn't going flying, the AFS will have a validity period, which we can't invalidate. In other words it's a confidence check that the aircraft is still good to go, but it'll only stay valid for a certain amount of time. So if it's sitting there for a week, you then have to do another

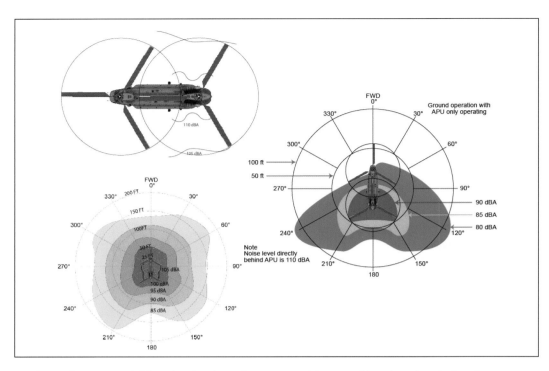

RIGHT Safety is paramount for Chinook engineers. This diagram provides cautionary information about the decibel levels around the aircraft when the APU is operating. *(Crown Copyright)*

BELOW Using a crane, engineers fit a rotor blade in Afghanistan; each rotor blade measures 27.5ft (8.3m) in length, and takes five or six men to lift manually. *(PRMAVIA Collection)*

service on it to re-establish safety levels and ensure that that aircraft is fit to fly. You can't do a servicing then push it into a hangar, leave it for a year, then pull it out and expect it to work. You have to maintain the level of serviceability.'

The BFS and AFS are there to ensure a continual standard of airworthiness, and they are implemented at home and abroad. Specific theatres also bring with them additional servicing considerations (see below for more details about desert and arctic issues), conveyed through 'supplements pages', as John Chadwick explains: 'What you have is your AFS and your BFS and you have what's called a supplements page. So whenever you go into a different environment that supplements page will carry different tasks that have to be carried out in line with your AFS and BFS. That's

another thing about aircraft maintenance. There are two types of maintenance: there are aircraft hours and calendar. So even when the aircraft is sat there doing nothing there's still regular maintenance to be performed. There's the top-up of the AFS and BFS, but there are also the calendar tasks, such as cleaning and monitoring tasks to prevent the aircraft degrading.'

The last points made here about maintenance based on aircraft hours and calendar dates is yet another aspect of keeping the Chinook in optimum readiness. This aspect of servicing means that the aircraft's components are not allowed to stray beyond their lifespan and remain in the aircraft. For example, in terms of calendar tasks, the aircraft battery is changed every 28 days, the rescue hoist hook every 91 days and the aircraft is to be washed every 28 days, even if it is sitting in a hangar.

Mark Lilley expands on the issues of component life, and also explains primary and minor maintenance, other significant staging points in the Chinook's maintenance life:

'Your components have all got a lifespan, which dictates whether they go for repair, reconditioning or are scrapped. So certain items will have a finite life; some things will be on a repair cycle, and some things will just simply be on condition, *ie* if they aren't broken then we can leave them on the aircraft. But then obviously we have routine maintenance on top of that. There are primaries, which can be set at flying-hour. In primary maintenance we're going to take the aircraft off the line for a certain number of days, and certain laid-down maintenance tasks are carried out. If there are any other tasks or faults that this aircraft has developed over a period of time, but we've lived with, we can then make a decision to repair those at that point. There are faults or damage on the aircraft that the aircrew will accept to a point, and these will exist until we get to the point when we can do maintenance on it. We might be doing some minor modifications to the aircraft within that work package. The aircraft is inspected at this time, so we'll take the majority of the role equipment off it; in theatre we'll also lift up the ballistic panels and some elements of the floor, do heavy cleaning. There's also what's known as a zonal survey, which is cleaning in effect.'

LEFT An RAF pilot inspects the rotor head on a Chinook helicopter during a pre-Afghanistan exercise; pilots must also perform pre-flight external checks of the airframe and major components. *(Crown Copyright)*

John Chadwick also expands on component life: 'Because the components have so many flying hours on them as well, if you have a component that breaks down, when you have to replace that component you very rarely have to get a brand new one – instead you'll get one that's been refurbished and has so many hours left on it. So the first thing that you're going to do is look at the aircraft and say, for example,

BELOW Chinooks undergo maintenance at the Fleetlands centre in Gosport, where the helicopters are sent for major overhauls by civilian defence contractors. In the foreground is a rotor assembly. *(PRMAVIA Collection)*

ABOVE A busy maintenance line in Afghanistan, including engine units and generators to provide power in the remote airstrip location. *(Simon Wheeler)*

"This has got 200 hours on it before it goes into a major service, so I'll have a transmission with as close as possible to 200 hours left on it, and then we can just change it again at the major service." Therefore the aircraft comes out of its major [service] with a max life transmission.'

With such a lot at stake in the use of components on the Chinook, it is key that the

BELOW Chinook ZD757 displays battle scars to the rear pylon, although the enemy fire did not inflict catastrophic damage on the engine itself. The engine is fitted with the EAPS system. *(PRMAVIA Collection)*

system is managed with total efficiency. Mark Lilley points out that: 'There's a computer system that manages all this for us, so that we don't overfly. The worst thing that can happen to us is overflying the life of a component, because you'd be sending an aircraft up that in effect isn't safe. So management of the component life is absolutely key.' Yet through their years of experience, and solid judgement, the engineers can also grant the component an official extension in time. For example, a Chinook's 600-hour aft vertical shaft could be extended by about 20 hours, or about 3% of its life, to bring it in line with a primary servicing, extending the life of that component to change it at a suitable maintenance opportunity. However, 'We can't apply extensions on to everything and extend a component for, say, 100%. We've got limits on what we can extend, but then we're referring those limits back to the Chinook PT (Project Team), the EAs (Engineering Authorities) and ultimately back to Boeing as well. So we've got scope to be flexible up to a point. Again, that process all needs managing and all needs controlling, and that's where a lot of the engineering managers – flight sergeants, warrant officers, and engineering officers – that's what they're looking at constantly, to make sure that we're not tipping the aircraft or the fleet into a dangerous condition.' John Chadwick adds: 'You aren't just looking at the risk of that component, there could be a number of other components on the aircraft that are already in an extension period. So there's a cumulative risk on that aircraft and you have to compare that aircraft against the whole fleet – how much risk is the whole fleet carrying with over-hours components? So what burden is that going to be ultimately for the stock we carry for major maintenance?'

The engineers can also apply lims (limitations) and ADFs (acceptable deferred faults) in their judgements about an aircraft's airworthiness. These enable the aircraft to fly with components that are essentially defective, but without affecting the flying safety of the aircraft. 'Say if it's something electrical, what'll happen is we'll come along and isolate the power supply, so we'll pull the circuit breaker and put a gag on it,' says Chris Collinson 'We put documentation into the aircraft's 700 [the aircraft's log book]

LEFT Another view
of engineers in
Afghanistan. The
front and rear rotor
blades have both been
removed for either
replacement or fitting
following shipment
of the aircraft. *(Simon
Wheeler)*

to make the aircrew aware that this particular
component, should they try to turn it on, isn't
going to work. It's an acceptable fault which is
not structurally significant, and if it's significant
then straight away it's changed.'

In a striking analogy, Chief Technician
Wheeler likened the process of maintaining
the Chinook fleet to 'juggling chainsaws',
a reference to both its complexity and its
challenging nature. The fact is that the
engineers have to ensure that the machines are
there ready to support operational or training
requirements, regardless of the engineering
demands. 'This is the job of the Fleet Planners,'
says Collinson. 'It's their job to look at major
component changes and minor servicing,
primaries and that kind of thing, and try to
schedule the aircraft usage. Unfortunately,
sometimes you can have five aircraft on the
line that are fully serviceable first thing on a
Monday, but by 0900 they're all US [unfit for
service] through faults.' Simon Wheeler adds:
'And obviously one problem is that we've got
three different marks of Chinook – we've got a
2, 3 and a 4 as well. ... Obviously you can't use
a Mk 3 for certain tasks; guys who are qualified
for a Mk 4 can't fly a Mk 2. So you have all
these added pressures; you can't just give the
aircrew a Chinook and say "Go fly", you've got
to think about what it's got to do, who's going
to fly it, where it's going to go, the number of
hours left on it – you can't have a transmission

ABOVE A crane is
used to haul a partially
dismantled Chinook into
position for the engineers
to work on. Chinooks
were some of the earliest
RAF air assets deployed
into the Afghan theatre.
(Simon Wheeler)

LEFT Off the coast
of Sierra Leone, an
engineer or pilot
inspects the pitot
tube/comms aerial
unit at the front of
the helicopter's nose.
(Crown Copyright)

Extreme environments

The Chinook's integration into the essentially logistical life of the British forces has meant that it has deployed to all conceivable manner of environments. Consequently the aircraft has had to be maintained in locations as diverse as Norway, California, Pakistan, the Balkans, the Falklands, Iraq and Afghanistan. Each different location brings its own set of flying requirements, as well as demands on the engineering requirements. The author asked the engineering team to explain some of the special considerations for two of the most demanding environments of all – desert and Arctic.

Desert

Arid environments have a defining ingredient – airborne particles. Grit and dust are, of course, present in most places, especially when stirred up by a powerful downwash. Yet in the desert, or in arid regions during the hottest months, sand and dust can have a profound effect on any aircraft, and the Chinook is no exception. Not only does the dust have a pervasive and detrimental effect on equipment; there is also the issue of sheer weight build-up. For these reasons alone, keeping the aircraft clean in theatre is a priority: 'One of the key things about operating in the desert is husbandry. Keeping the aircraft as clean as possible, wiping all the shiny bits, the dampers, the undercarriage. It's a headache, but if it gets dirty the grit and the dirt get into the components and the aircraft becomes more and more US. Although it seems like all we're doing is cleaning all the time, it's key to keeping the helicopter serviceable. The type of sand abroad is different from the UK – you can go from talcum powder to sand-blasting material.'

The cleaning regimen in desert areas ultimately demands that the aircraft is vacuumed out every 24 hours. In addition, extreme heat also affects the performance of various aviation fluids, requiring components such as transmissions to be drained and flushed and re-oiled to get the correct levels of lubrication. The aircraft's bearings and swashplates also require more lubricants. Yet at the same time, says Simon Wheeler, 'Desert conditions also affect vibration levels, because you get sand build-up on the blades. Because the heat makes the oil leak, the oil spreads along

ABOVE An entire aft rotor pylon is removed from a Chinook for servicing. Both the engines and the infrared jammer units on the side have been covered during maintenance. *(Crown Copyright)*

cap of, say, two hours on a transmission and send it off on a four-hour sortie, because after two hours it's got to stop somewhere and then you've got to change the transmission in the middle of a field – which has happened.'

Despite the multiple, and frequently competing, demands that the Chinook engineers have to face, the fact remains that the Chinook fleet continues to be one of the most dynamically active of the RAF's air assets. The thousands of hours of sorties flown in Afghanistan, Odiham and other locations around the world are entirely dependent on the efforts of the engineering community.

BELOW Locations and fuel capacities of the Chinook's port and starboard fuel tanks. *(Crown Copyright)*

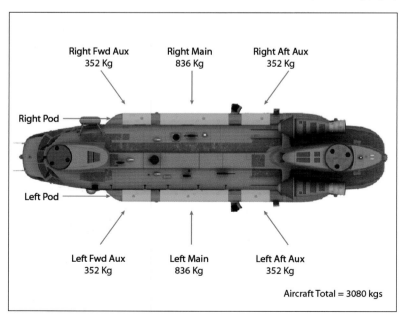

Right Fwd Aux
352 Kg

Right Main
836 Kg

Right Aft Aux
352 Kg

Right Pod

Left Pod

Left Fwd Aux
352 Kg

Left Main
836 Kg

Left Aft Aux
352 Kg

Aircraft Total = 3080 kgs

the blades and the sand sticks to it, and in the shafts too, and produces additional vibration' – another reason why cleaning of the Chinook must be diligently maintained.

Sand and dust are particularly abrasive materials, and their erosive effect is most aggressively directed at the rotor blades, which have to endure millions of tiny impacts with every sortie. Erosion is the main problem for the rotor blades, and all sorts of measures are taken to try to prevent damage. Although the blades are protected against erosion through the fitting of erosion caps, the engineers also apply 28in (71cm) strips of polyurethane 'sacrificial tape', as an extra level of protection.

As well as air-blown detritus, the engineers also have to deal with the foreign bodies carried on board the aircraft by troops, vehicles and other internal loads. Chris Collinson:

'It's not only about what's around the aircraft, it's also about what the troops bring into the aircraft. Everyone thinks of Afghanistan being a reasonably arid country, but at times it absolutely chucks it down; the troops will go out and do a particular job, plunging through a poppy field or something like that, and they'll drag all of it back on to the aircraft on their boots – it's as if they've taken the whole field on to the aircraft and sat

down in their seats. When they depart they leave their trails all over the pan, and then it is up to us to rip all that role equipment out and give it a good jet wash. Unfortunately, relating to the MERT side of things – certainly in the early days when we didn't have any special kit – casualties were brought on board the aircraft, and after that you're cleaning up blood and body parts. We also need to warn people a lot further down the line, because when these aircraft eventually come back from theatre, more often than not they end up going down to Fleetlands [the Vector Aerospace servicing centre in Gosport].

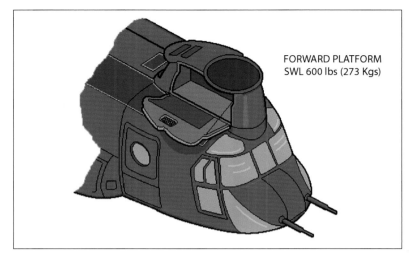

FORWARD PLATFORM
SWL 600 lbs (273 Kgs)

ABOVE **The forward work platform, used when servicing the forward rotor unit and its associated transmission.** *(Crown Copyright)*

LEFT **The Chinook's rotor blades, while resilient features of the aircraft, require constant inspection for any cracks, battle damage and the effects of airborne particles.** *(Crown Copyright)*

BELOW **The workings of one of the rotor pylons are exposed during maintenance; the rotor driveshaft runs straight down from the rotor hub to the transmission.** *(Crown Copyright)*

Those people at Fleetlands will strip the aircraft down to a lower level, and they need to know, if they're lifting up floor panels, what dust and contaminants might be lurking beneath them. They need to be correctly dressed, because they don't want to be breathing in God knows what.'

Another issue highlighted by the group was that the metal of the aircraft could become so hot in desert areas that touching the surfaces with bare skin would result in a burn. For this reason gloves have to be worn, in turn affecting manual dexterity. Metal components might also swell up in the heat, prohibiting them from being fitted, and requiring submersion in water to bring them back down to a usable temperature.

Arctic

At the other environmental extreme are Arctic conditions, most frequently encountered when the Chinook is deployed on exercise to Norway. For the engineers, sub-zero conditions make

even the simplest task an extended exercise, as the climate is as hard on the men as it is on the airframe. For example, says Mark Lilley: 'We have to wrap the aircraft up in covers to protect it, so before the aircrew can even go flying we could have been out there for an hour already just taking the covers off. For every single blade we've got what we call a blade sock fitted; there's also a cover over the top of the heads, the cockpit is covered up, the windscreens are covered up, we fit skis to the aircraft, there are ropes and other pieces. Snow has to be removed from the airframe. All this before that mechanic has even started his flight servicing. So sometimes the aircrew might want to go flying at 0800 in the morning, you can be working on it from five in the morning to get it ready. And obviously when they land, we have to reverse the process, cocooning the aircraft back up again.'

As a general rule, every engineering job performed in Arctic conditions takes two or three times longer than the same task performed in a temperate zone. To protect those exposed to the elements, one team of engineers typically works on the aircraft, while another team stays warm in a vehicle or building, the teams swapping about every 10 to 15 minutes. The oil, for example, has to be brought up to the correct temperature and viscosity. (Jamie Pearce notes: 'There's also a document called the Release to Service, which states the temperatures at which you can operate, giving a minimum and maximum temperature.') Of course, the engineers can work in a controlled environment, such as a hangar, but even that can bring its own issues, as Mark Lilley explains: 'You imagine just a simple task, like you've been advised to go out to the aircraft and start the aircraft. You've got a downwash of about 40–50mph from the rotors, roughly. Obviously you then have that downwash in −20°, and then you have the wind chill on that. As well as issues with manual dexterity, just moving around is a problem with all the kit on. In Norway, there were times when we were bagging and tagging the aircraft in a hangar where it's nice and warm, and then you drag the aircraft outside and everything shrinks in the cold. Because of this you suddenly get leaks.' Matt Baker adds: 'You also get condensation building up inside the aircraft; then that condensation, which was created in that warm environment, freezes inside the aircraft when it goes outside. So you have internal parts all covered with ice.'

Controlling ice build-up is a constant challenge, but additional chances of damage are also a possibility in the Arctic environment. Chris Collinson: 'The anti-icing that's on the aircraft is quite limited. We've got heated windscreens, and there's a cabin and cockpit heater, which are, I suppose, similar to the heater blower on a car. On fixed-wing aircraft, there are anti-icing panels and that sort of thing, but there's nothing like that on the blades at all. Any snow and ice we have to clear off beforehand, and if the crew observe any ice or snow build-up during flight then they might have to consider putting their aircraft down. There's also, unfortunately, another problem due to the nature of the places where the pilots land: there's more of a chance that the aircrew will come back with parts of the aircraft missing, because when they go flying around they pick a spot to land, and quite often they end up landing in quite deep snow. In somewhere like Norway, there's a lot of granite out there. You can land in the snow, but what the crew don't realise is that they've stuck a leg between two bits of rock. The result is that the helicopter comes back without a leg, or with a big hole in the bottom from fence posts and other objects.'

The team pointed out that in many cases

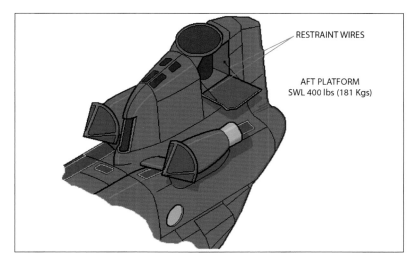

RESTRAINT WIRES

AFT PLATFORM
SWL 400 lbs (181 Kgs)

the crew will actually be unaware of damage incurred. For this reason, the engineers have to perform regular close inspections to ensure such damage doesn't go unseen.

Chinook engineers pride themselves on being an adaptive and professional force, and their rather expeditionary mindset is very clear in interviews. The Chinook fleet is massively in demand, whether in training or on operations, and this military facility is squarely dependent on those who can maintain these aircraft. Without their efforts, essential capabilities such as front-line resupply and medical evacuations would be just as impossible as they would without a flying crew.

ABOVE The aft pylon work platform – the weights refer to the maximum load that can be placed on the platform; anything more requires scaffolding or some other external platform. (Crown Copyright)

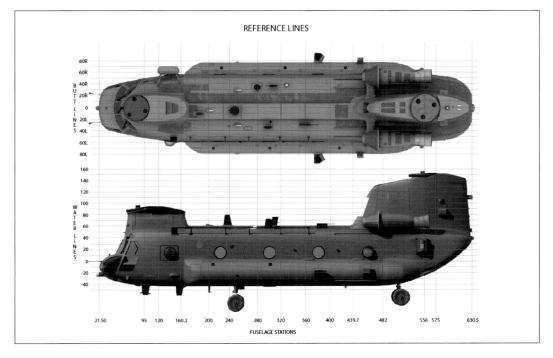

LEFT A engineering diagram that allows Chinook engineers to identify precisely where faults are found on the airframe, and pass what are effectively coordinates to other engineers. (Crown Copyright)

Glossary of acronyms

AMM – Aircraft maintenance mechanic.
ACH – Attack Cargo Helicopter.
ADF – Acceptable deferred fault or automatic direction finder.
AFCS – Automatic flight control system.
AFS – After Flight Servicing.
AI – Attitude indicator.
AMS Aircraft management section or aircraft management system.
AoR – Area of operations.
APU – Auxiliary power unit.
ASI – Air speed indicator.
ATVA – Adaptive tuned vibration absorber.
BFS – Before Flight Servicing.
CAAS – Common avionics architecture system.
CDNU – Control and display navigation unit.
DAFCS – Digital advanced flight control system.
DAS – Defensive aids suite.
DECU – Digital electronic control unit.
DFC – Distinguished Flying Cross.
DNVG – Display night-vision goggles.
EAPS – Engine air particle separator system or engine advanced protection system.
EAW – Expeditionary Air Wing.
ECL – Engine condition levers.
EOD – Explosive ordnance disposal.
ERT – Emergency Response Team.
ESU – Electronic sequencing unit.
FADEC – Full authority digital engine control.
FARE – Forward air refuelling equipment.
FLIR – Forward-looking infrared system.
FOB – Forward operating base.
fpm – Feet per minute.
GPS – Global positioning system.
HLS – Helicopter landing site.
HMA – Hydromechanical assembly.
HRF – Helmand Reaction Force.
HSI – Horizontal situation indicator.
ICOM – Intelligence communication.
IFF – Identification friend or foe.
IFOR – Implementation Force.

ILS – Instrument landing system.
IRT – Incident response team.
ISAF – International Security Assistance Force.
JHF(A) – Joint Helicopter Force (Afghanistan).
JOC – Joint operations centre.
JTAC – Joint terminal attack controller.
KAF – Kandahar Airfield.
LCT – Longitudinal cyclic trim.
Medevac – Medical evacuation.
MERT – Medical emergency response team.
MFD – Multi-function display.
MFOS – Multi-function operator's seat.
MoD – Ministry of Defence.
NEP – Night-enhancement package.
NR – Rotor blade speed as a percentage of rpm.
NVG – Night-vision goggles.
OCU – Operational Conversion Unit.
P&W – Pratt & Whitney.
PB – Patrol base.
PGM – Precision-guided munition.
POW – Prisoner of war.
PTIT – Power turbine inlet temperature.
PTU – Power transfer units.
Rad alt – Radar altimeter.
Rat packs – Ration packs.
RPG – Rocket-propelled grenade.
rpm – Revolutions per minute.
RWR – Radar warning receiver.
SAFIRE – Small-arms fire.
SAM – Surface-to-air missile.
SF – Special Forces.
SHF – Support Helicopter Force.
shp – Shaft horsepower.
SOP – Standard operating procedures.
TACAN – Tactical air navigation.
UORs – Urgent operational requirements.
USL – Underslung load.
VCP – Vehicle checkpoint.
VSI – Vertical speed indicator.
WSO – Weapons support officer.

Index